Windows™ Programming PowerPack

Windows™ Programming PowerPack

Jeffrey D. Clark

SAMS PUBLISHING

A Division of Prentice Hall Computer Publishing
11711 North College, Carmel, Indiana 46032 USA

FIRST EDITION
FIRST PRINTING—1992

International Standard Book Number: 0-672-30129-6

Library of Congress Catalog Card Number: 92-74183

95 94 93 92 4 3 2 1

Interpretation of the printing code: the rightmost double-digit number is the year of the book's printing; the rightmost single-digit, the number of the book's printing. For example, a printing code of 92-1 shows that the first printing of the book occurred in 1992.

Composed in AGaramond and MCPdigital
by Prentice Hall Computer Publishing

Printed in the United States of America

Trademarks

Publisher
Richard K. Swadley

Managing Editor
Neweleen A. Trebnik

Acquisitions Editor
Gregory Croy

Development Editor
Stacy Hiquet

Production Editor
Tad Ringo

Editors
Cheri Clark
Grant Fairchild
Gayle Johnson

Editorial Coordinators
Rebecca S. Freeman
Bill Whitmer

Editorial Assistants
Rosemarie Graham
Lori Keley

Technical Editor
Bruce Graves

Cover Designer
Jean Bisesi

Production Director
Jeff Valler

Production Manager
Corinne Walls

Imprint Manager
Matthew Morrill

Book Designer
Michele Laseau

Production Analyst
Mary Beth Wakefield

Proofreading/Indexing Coordinator
Joelynn Gifford

Indexer
Sharon Hilgenberg

Production
Christine Cook
Lisa Daugherty
Chuck Hutchinson
Roger Morgan
Michelle Self
Greg Simsic
Angie Trzepacz

OVERVIEW

TABLE OF CONTENTS

About the Author

Jeffrey D. Clark is president of Mycrowynn Corporation, a firm that specializes in Microsoft Windows consulting and programming. He is the author of *Windows Programmer's Guide to OLE/DDE.*

INTRODUCTION

The Windows Programming PowerPack is based on the programming library, Drover's Professional Toolbox for Windows. Drover's Toolbox is a very large, feature-rich product that encompasses thousands of hours of program development. The Windows Programming PowerPack is a subset of Drover's Toolbox, and even though PowerPack is only a subset of the Toolbox, it consists of hundreds of hours of program development.

I consider products like Drover's Professional Toolbox a necessity to wisely developing Windows applications. The programming time saved from using development libraries quickly pays for the development libraries.

The Windows Programming PowerPack enables you to survey some of the features of Drover's Toolbox. The Windows Programming PowerPack includes custom controls that can be used in dialog boxes and windows, and functions that interface with the custom controls and provide low-level access to system functions. Using the functions and controls is as easy as using the existing Windows controls and API.

This book consists of five chapters and one appendix. The first chapter discusses using PowerPack. (By its length, it is easy to determine that PowerPack is easy to use.) The second chapter describes the custom controls and functions that interface with the controls. Chapter 3 covers functions not related to controls. Chapter 4 is a message reference for the custom controls. The final chapter describes structures used in functions from previous chapters.

The appendix is a source code listing of an example program that implements many of the PowerPack functions and all of the PowerPack controls. This program is written in Microsoft C 7.0, but can be compiled using any C compiler that generates Windows executables. The functions and controls are also accessible from SQL Windows, Actor, and ToolBook.

System Requirements

The PowerPack can be used with any PC that can compile Windows applications. This varies from compiler to compiler, but is generally an 80386 PC with 2 to 4 M of RAM. Any C or C++ compiler that can generate Windows applications can be used with PowerPack. This includes Borland C++ 2.0 or later. The example program included on the source disk was compiled on a Gateway 2000 486/33 with 16 M of RAM using Microsoft C/C++ 7.0 and Microsoft Windows 3.1.

1

Using the PowerPack

This section describes the contents of the PowerPack diskette and describes how to interface PowerPack routines from your Microsoft C programs. PowerPack also interfaces with other development environments, including Actor, WindowsMaker, Borland C++, ToolBook, and SQLWindows.

Introduction to PowerPack

PowerPack consists of a Dynamic Link Library (DLL). The aim of this library is to enhance the functionality of the Microsoft Windows Software Development Kit (SDK) and to simplify the task of creating professional, high-quality Windows applications. Using PowerPack controls and functions, developers can minimize programming overhead and begin building applications far sooner than if they were to develop the functionality themselves. Developers who are new to Windows will find that PowerPack drastically reduces the normal learning curve, enabling them to be productive in a fraction of the usual time involved in learning a new development environment.

PowerPack functions have been designed to appear as much like Windows SDK functions as possible. The naming conventions are similar, and where C runtime functions have been converted to accept far pointers (for instance, the string handling functions), the function name has been capitalized. For example, `StrCpy` is the far pointer version of `strcpy`. Where additional functions have been added, full names have been used to conform to the Windows naming conventions. Notice that runtime functions `atoi` and `atol` have been renamed to `StringToInt` and `StringToLong`, respectively.

PowerPack also contains 10 useful controls that represent years of development time.

USING POWERPACK IN AN APPLICATION

The following steps are required to utilize the features of PowerPack with a C application. Some of them are automatically performed by the installation program, if used.

- PowerPack .DLL files must be placed in the directory of the application, or in a directory in the search path (as set by the SET PATH statement). Windows needs to find the DLLs whenever the application program references functions within them. DLLs are sometimes placed in the main Windows directory.

- powerpak.h, the PowerPack header file, should be placed in a directory in the current include path (as set by the SET INCLUDE statement). This file is referenced by your .C and .DLG files, and the compiler must be able to find it. The file can be placed in the same directories as the SDK header files (normally \WINDEV\INCLUDE).
- The import library, POWERPAK.LIB, should be placed in a directory in the current library path (as set by the SET LIB statement). These files are used by the linker. The library files may be placed in the same directory as the SDK libraries, usually \WINDEV\LIB.
- Every .C and .DLG file that uses PowerPack functions or controls must include the file powerpak.h. This file contains the function prototypes, data structure definitions, and other information required to utilize PowerPack.
- The link statement for the application must link in the import library for the PowerPack DLLs. The import library for POWERPAK.DLL is POWERPAK.LIB.

  For instance, the command

  ```
  LINK myprog,/NOD /NOE,,llibcew libw powerpak,
  myprog
  ```

  links the import libraries for the PowerPack DLLs.
- Before any PowerPack function or control is accessed, the function `InitToolBox` must be called. This function initializes the libraries and registers all the control window types. This function may be called only once in an application, and is usually called in the window initialization portion of the program.

InitToolBox

This function initializes the PowerPack controls and functions, and calls the PowerPack DLL.

Syntax: `BOOL InitToolBox(hInst)`

Parameter: `hInst`

Type: `HANDLE`

Description: The instance handle of the calling program.

Return Value: The return value is TRUE if the PowerPack is successfully initialized.

The source code for the sample application included with the PowerPack (POWER.EXE) provides excellent examples of the initializing requirements.

Note: The PowerPack DLL is model-independent, but it is recommended that either the small or medium model libraries be used for Windows development. Using the large model library causes all code segments in the executable to be fixed in memory, causing Windows to excessively swap the code segments to disk when under heavy load.

2

Controls and Control Functions

The Date Control (tbDate)

tbDate is a formatted date control that supports several common formats. The character used to separate the day, month, and year (- in the following examples) is taken from the Windows setup. By default, the current date is loaded into the control when it is first displayed.

The tbDate control performs data validation as the user enters new data. An EN_INVALIDDATA message is sent to the parent if the control contains an invalid date. The parent must then determine the proper course of action, but the date field usually clears to give the user another chance.

You must use the standard **SetDlgItemText** and **GetDlgItemText** API calls (or the WM_GETTEXT and WM_SETTEXT messages) to set or retrieve the date from the control.

No conversion is performed for Julian dates regarding the Clavian correction in 1701 or the 3-day Gregorian adjustment in 1752.

DATE DIALOG STATEMENT

The following statement places a tbDate control in the resource file:

```
CONTROL "", id, "tbDate",  style, x, y, width, height
```

id — Integer value specifying the unique resource ID.

style — Integer value containing any combination of the standard WS_ styles and the following tbDate styles:

- DS_CENTURY
- DS_DEFCENTURY
- DS_DDMMYY
- DS_DDMONYY
- DS_MMDDYY
- DS_SPIN
- DS_YYMMDD

These styles are described more fully in the next section.

x,y — Integer values specifying the x and y coordinates of the top-left corner of the control. The horizontal units are 1/4 of the dialog base width unit; the vertical units are 1/8 of the dialog base height unit.

`width` Integer value specifying the width of the control. The width unit is 1/4 of the dialog base width unit.

`height` Integer value specifying the height of the control. The height unit is 1/8 of the dialog base height unit.

DATE CONTROL STYLES

The following styles are valid for the `tbDate` control:

`DS_CENTURY` Specifies that all date styles include the full 4-digit year. By default, only the last two digits of the year are displayed.

`DS_DEFCENTURY` Specifies that the default century format is taken from the Windows setup.

`DS_DDMONYY` Display and entry of the date are in the form DD-MON-YY. October 1, 1992 is displayed as `01-OCT-92`. When entering the date, the user enters `O` when the cursor is over the middle section of the date field and the `OCT` portion automatically appears. If the month is July, three presses of `J` are required (first `JAN`, then `JUN`, and finally `JUL` is displayed).

`DS_DDMMYY` Display and entry of the date are in the form DD-MM-YY. October 1, 1992 is displayed as `01-10-92`.

`DS_MMDDYY` Display and entry of the date are in the form MM-DD-YY. October 1, 1992 is displayed as `10-01-92`.

`DS_SPIN` A spin button is placed to the right side of the date control, allowing the user to change the date with the mouse.

DS_YYMMDD	Display and entry of the date are in the form YY-MM-DD. October 1, 1992 is displayed as 92-10-01.

DATE CONTROL HOT KEYS

The date control automatically includes two hot keys for entering a date:

TABLE 2.1. DATE CONTROL HOT KEYS.

Key	*Purpose*
F2	Loads the current date into the control.
F4	Displays a pop-up calendar from which the user can select a date.

DATE CONTROL EXAMPLE

The following resource statement creates a tbDate control with the MM-DD-YYYY format:

```
CONTROL "", IDD_DATE, "tbDate",
    WS_CHILD ¦ WS_BORDER ¦ DS_MMDDYY ¦      DS_CENTURY,
    30, 30, 80, 25
```

The following code retrieves the date entered by the user:

```
GetDlgItemText(hWnd, IDD_DATE, DateBuffer, 10);
```

DATE CONTROL RELATED FUNCTIONS

Not all the following functions are needed to use the tbDate control effectively, but they are useful when manipulating the dates entered.

TABLE 2.2. DATE FUNCTIONS.

Function	*Description*
`DateAddDays`	Adds days to a date structure.
`DateDMYtoJulian`	Converts a day, month, year to a Julian data type.
`DateDMYToString`	Converts a day, month, year to a date string.
`DateGetCurrentDate`	Gets and formats the current date.
`DateGetDlgItemFormat`	Gets the format of a `tbDate` control (dialog version).
`DateGetFormat`	Gets the format of a `tbDate` control (child window version).
`DateGetWeekday`	Returns the day of the week given a particular date.
`DateIntIsValid`	Determines if a date is valid.
`DateJulianToDMY`	Converts a Julian data type to a day, month, year.
`DateSetDlgItemFormat`	Sets the format of a `tbDate` control (dialog version).
`DateSetDlgItemRange`	Sets a range of valid dates for the control (dialog version).
`DateSetFormat`	Sets the format of a `tbDate` control (child window version).
`DateSetRange`	Sets a range of valid dates for the control.
`DateStringIsValid`	Determines whether a date string contains a legal date.
`DateStringToDMY`	Converts a date string to day, month, year.
`DateSubtractDates`	Subtracts dates from a date structure.

DateAddDays

The `DateAddDays` function adds the specified number of days to a valid date.

Syntax: `LPDATE  DateAddDays(lpDate1,iNoDays)`

Parameter: `lpDate1`

Type: `LPDATE`

Description: Points to a structure that contains the day, month, and year.

Parameter: `iNoDays`

Type: `int`

Description: The number of days to add to the date. Can be negative.

Return value: The return value is a pointer to the date structure.

DateDMYtoJulian

The `DateDMYtoJulian` function translates a date structure to a Julian date.

Syntax: `LONG  DateDMYtoJulian(lpDate)`

Parameter: `lpDate`

Type: `LPDATE`

Description: Points to a structure that contains the day, month, and year.

Return value: The return value is the Julian date expressed as a long integer.

DateDMYToString

The `DateDMYToString` function translates a date structure to a string date in the specified format.

Syntax: `LPSTR  DateDMYToString(lpDate,lpString,lpFormat)`

Parameter: `lpDate`

Type: `LPDATE`

Description: Points to a structure containing the day, month, and year.

Parameter: `lpString`

Type: `LPSTR`

Description: Points to the string that receives the formatted date.

Parameter: `lpFormat`

Type: `LPDATEFORMAT`

Description: Points to a structure containing fields that define the format for the date.

Return value: The return value is a pointer to the string date.

DateGetDlgItemFormat

The `DateGetDlgItemFormat` function retrieves the current date format from a date control.

Syntax: `BOOL  DateGetDlgItemFormat(hDlg,iID,lpDateFmt)`

Parameter: `hDlg`

Type: `HWND`

Description: The window handle of the dialog box.

Parameter: `iID`

Type: `int`

Description: The control ID of the `bDate` control.

Parameter: `lpDateFmt`

Type: `LPDATEFORMAT`

Description: Points to a structure where the date control's format information will be written.

Return value: The return value is TRUE if the function is successfully completed. FALSE is returned if the format can't be obtained.

Comments: This function is defined as a macro in powerpak.h.

DateGetFormat

The `DateGetFormat` function retrieves the current date format from a date control.

Syntax: `BOOL  DateGetFormat(hDateWnd,lpDateFmt)`

Parameter: `hDateWnd`

Type: `HWND`

Description: The window handle of the `tbDate` control.

Parameter: `lpDateFmt`

Type: `LPDATEFORMAT`

Description: Points to a structure to which the date control's format information will be written.

Return value: The return value is TRUE if the function is completed successfully. FALSE is returned if the format can't be obtained.

Comments: If the `tbDate` control is part of a dialog box, the `DateGetDlgItemFormat` function (actually a macro) can be used.

DateGetWeekday

The `DateGetWeekday` function determines the weekday of a given date.

Syntax: `LPSTR  DateGetWeekday(lpDate,szDay)`

Parameter: `lpDate`

Type: `LPDATE`

Description: Points to a structure that contains the day, month, and year.

Parameter: `szDay`

Type: `LPSTR`

Description: Points to a string to which the day of the week will be written.

Return value: The return value is a pointer to `szDay`.

Comments: The string placed in `szDay` is the literal weekday name (Saturday). The first letter is always capitalized; the rest are lowercase.

DateIntIsValid

The `DateIntIsValid` function determines whether the date in a structure is valid.

Syntax: `BOOL  DateIntIsValid(lpDate)`

Parameter: `lpDate`

Type: `LPDATE`

Description: Points to a structure that contains the day, month, and year.

Return value: The return value is TRUE if the date in the structure is valid. FALSE is returned if it isn't.

Comments: Because the other date-handling functions assume the date in a structure is valid, this function should be used before the structure is passed to one of the others.

DateJulianToDMY

The `DateJulianToDMY` function converts a Julian date to a day/month/year date structure.

Syntax: `VOID  DateJulianToDMY(lJulian,lpDate)`

Parameter: `lJulian`

Type: `LONG`

Description: The Julian (integer) date.

Parameter: `lpDate`

Type: `LPDATE`

Description: A pointer to a structure where the day, month, and year will be placed.

DateSetDlgItemFormat

The `DateSetDlgItemFormat` function sets the format of a date control.

Syntax: `BOOL  DateSetDlgItemFormat(hDlg,iID,lpDateFmt)`

Parameter: `hDlg`

Type: `HWND`

Description: The window handle of the dialog box that contains the `tbDate` control.

Parameter: `iID`

Type: `int`

Description: The control ID of the `tbDate` control.

Parameter: `lpDateFmt`

Type: `LPDATEFORMAT`

Description: Points to a structure that defines the formatting parameters for the date control.

Return value: The return value is TRUE if the format is set successfully.

Comments: This function is defined as a macro in powerpak.h.

DateSetDlgItemRange

The `DateSetDlgItemRange` function sets the legal range of a date control.

Syntax: `BOOL  DateSetDlgItemRange(hDlg,iID,Min,Max)`

Parameter: `hDlg`

Type: `HWND`

Description: The window handle of the dialog box that contains the `tbDate` control.

Parameter: `iID`

Type: `int`

Description: The contol ID of the `tbDate` control.

Parameter: `Min`

Type: `LPDATE`

Description: Points to a structure that defines the earliest valid date.

Parameter: `Max`

Type: `LPDATE`

Description: Points to a structure that defines the latest valid date.

Return value: The return value is TRUE if the range is set successfully.

Comments: If the `Min` parameter specifies a date later than `Max`, the function returns FALSE and no range is set.

DateSetFormat

The `DateSetFormat` function sets the format of a date control.

Syntax: `BOOL  DateSetFormat(hDateWnd,lpDateFmt)`

Parameter: `hDateWnd`

Type: `HWND`

Description: The window handle of the `tbDate` control.

Parameter: `lpDateFmt`

Type: `LPDATEFORMAT`

Description: Points to a structure that contains the formatting parameters for the `tbDate` control.

Return value: The return value is TRUE if the format is set successfully.

Comments: If the `tbDate` control is part of a dialog box, you can use the `DateSetDlgItemFormat` function (actually a macro).

DATESETRANGE

The `DateSetRange` function sets the legal range of a date control.

Syntax: `BOOL  DateSetRange(hDateWnd,Min,Max)`

Parameter: `hDateWnd`

Type: `HWND`

Description: The window handle of the `tbDate` control.

Parameter: `Min`

Type: `LPDATE`

Description: Points to a structure that defines the earliest valid date.

Parameter: `Max`

Type: `LPDATE`

Description: Points to a structure that defines the latest valid date.

Return value: The return value is TRUE if the range is set successfully.

Comments: If the `Min` parameter specifies a date later than `Max`, the function returns FALSE and no range is set.

DATESTRINGISVALID

The `DateStringIsValid` function determines whether a date string represents a valid date.

Syntax: `BOOL  DateStringIsValid(lpDateStr,lpDateFormat)`

Parameter: `lpDateStr`

Type: `LPSTR`

Description: Points to a string that contains the date string.

Parameter: `lpDateFormat`

Type: `LPDATEFORMAT`

Description: Points to a structure that contains the formatting parameters to which the string date must conform.

Return value: The return value is TRUE if the string contains a valid date, FALSE if it doesn't.

DATESTRINGTODMY

The `DateStringToDMY` function converts a date string to a day/month/year date structure.

Syntax: `VOID  DateStringToDMY(lpDateStr,lpDate,lpDateFmt)`

Parameter: `lpDateStr`

Type: `LPSTR`

Description: Points to a string that contains a valid date string.

Parameter: `lpDate`

Type: `LPDATE`

Description: Points to a structure that receives the day, month, and year.

Parameter: `lpDateFmt`

Type: `LPDATEFORMAT`

Description: Points to a structure that defines the formatting parameters to which the date string must conform.

Comments: If the date string passed to this function isn't valid, the contents of the `lpDate` structure are highly unpredictable.

DateSubtractDates

The `DateSubtractDates` function subtracts two date structures, returning the number of days between them.

Syntax: `LONG  DateSubtractDates(lpDate1,lpDate2)`

Parameter: `lpDate1`

Type: `LPDATE`

Description: Points to a structure that contains the day, month, and year of the first date.

Parameter: `lpDate2`

Type: `LPDATE`

Description: Points to a structure that contains the day, month, and year of the second date.

Return value: The return value is the number of days, positive or negative, that occur between the two specified dates.

Edit Control (tbEdit)

The `tbEdit` control is a single-line edit control that permits the use of the Insert key to insert or overlay data in the edit field.

Note: Since the release of Windows 3.0 (with the exception of the insert/overlay capabilities), the functionality of this control has been matched by the standard Windows edit control. The control is included to maintain compatibility with existing ToolBox applications.

EDIT DIALOG STATEMENT

The following statement places a `tbEdit` control in the resource file:

```
CONTROL "", id, "tbEdit", style, x, y, width, height
```

- `id` Integer value specifying the unique resource ID.
- `style` Integer value that contains any combination of the standard `WS_` or `ES_` styles.
- `x,y` Integer values that specify the x and y coordinates of the top-left corner of the control. The horizontal units are 1/4 of the dialog base width unit; the vertical units are 1/8 of the dialog base height unit.
- `width` Integer value that specifies the width of the control. The width unit is 1/4 of the dialog base width unit.
- `height` Integer value that specifies the height of the control. The height unit is 1/8 of the dialog base height unit.

EDIT CONTROL STYLES

The `tbEdit` control supports all the styles supported by the Windows `Edit` class, with the exception of `ES_MULTILINE` and `ES_AUTOHSCROLL`.

EDIT CONTROL MESSAGES

The `tbEdit` control supports all the styles supported by the Windows `Edit` class, with the exception of those messages pertaining to the multi-line style.

THE FLOAT CONTROL (TBFLOAT)

The `tbFloat` control provides validated entry of floating-point numbers. Both the formatting of the field and the range of valid entries can be specified by the application. The entry of any characters other than numbers and the decimal point is locked out by this control.

FLOAT DIALOG STATEMENT

The following statement places a `tbFloat` control in the resource file:

```
CONTROL mask, id, "tbFloat", style, x, y, width, height
```

`mask` String that specifies the size of the float field. Specifically, the number of digits to the right and left of the decimal point is specified by placing the proper number of nines in the string, followed by a decimal point, followed by a nine for each digit to the right of the decimal point. (See the Float Control Examples section to follow.)

`id` Integer value that specifies the unique resource ID.

`style` Integer value that contains any combination of the standard `WS_` styles and the following float-specific styles:

```
FS_MONEY
FS_SEPARATOR
```

These styles are described more fully in the next section.

`x,y` Integer values that specify the x and y coordinates based in the top-left corner of the control. The horizontal units are 1/4 of the dialog base width unit; the vertical units are 1/8 of the dialog base height unit.

`width` Integer value that specifies the width of the control. The width unit is 1/4 of the dialog base width unit.

`height` Integer value that specifies the height of the control. The height unit is 1/8 of the dialog base height unit.

FLOAT CONTROL STYLES

The following styles can be used with the float control:

`FS_MONEY` This style indicates that a dollar sign should precede the value. The dollar sign is placed automatically as soon as the user begins to enter a number. The user is unable to delete the dollar sign.

`FS_SEPARATOR` This style indicates that the float field is to include commas (45,343.12). These commas appear automatically as the user enters the number.

FLOAT CONTROL EXAMPLES

The following resource statement creates a float control that accepts a number with seven digits to the left and three digits to the right of the decimal point. It has commas but isn't a money field.

```
CONTROL "9999999.999", "tbFloat", IDD_FLOATFIELD,
   WS_TABSTOP ¦ WS_BORDER ¦ WS_CHILD ¦
   FS_SEPARATOR, 10, 10, 100, 12
```

The following code then sets the range of the control from –100.00 to 7,000,000.00. This code typically is placed in the `WM_INITDIALOG` section of the dialog procedure.

```
FloatSetDlgItemRange(hWnd, IDD_FLOATFIELD, -100.0,
    7000000.0);
```

FLOAT CONTROL FUNCTIONS

The `tbFloat` control is supported by the following API calls. The function prototypes for these functions are contained in powerpak.h. All functions are declared as `FAR` and `PASCAL`.

TABLE 2.3. FLOAT CONTROL FUNCTIONS.

Function	*Description*
`FloatFormatString`	Creates a format mask according to specifications.
`FloatGetDlgItemRange`	Same as `FloatGetRange`, but takes dialog ID as parameter.
`FloatGetDlgItemValue`	Same as `FloatGetValue`, but takes dialog ID as parameter.
`FloatGetFormat`	Gets the currency symbol, decimal point, and separator characters.
`FloatGetRange`	Retrieves the current minimum and maximum ranges for the float control.
`FloatGetValue`	Retrieves the value of the float field as a double.
`FloatSetDlgItemRange`	Same as `FloatSetRange`, but takes dialog ID as parameter.
`FloatSetDlgItemValue`	Same as `FloatSetValue`, but takes dialog ID as parameter.
`FloatSetFormat`	Sets the currency symbol, decimal point, and separator characters.
`FloatSetMask`	Specifies a new mask for the float control.
`FloatSetRange`	Specifies the minimum and maximum acceptable values for the float control. The user is prevented from entering numbers out of this range.

Function	*Description*
`FloatSetStyle`	Specifies a new style for the float control.
`FloatSetValue`	Loads the specified value into the float field.

FLOATFORMATSTRING

The `FloatFormatString` function formats a floating-point value into a formatted string.

Syntax: `LPSTR FloatFormatString(fVal,szBuffer,bSeparator, bMoney,iDecimalPlaces)`

Parameter: `fVal`

Type: `double`

Description: The value to convert to a string.

Parameter: `szBuffer`

Type: `LPSTR`

Description: A pointer to the string that receives the formatted number.

Parameter: `bSeparator`

Type: `BOOL`

Description: Specifies whether a comma should be used to separate thousands in the number (1,234.44).

TRUE	Use the comma separator.
FALSE	Don't use the separator.

Parameter: `bMoney`

Type: `BOOL`

Description: Specifies whether the number should be formatted as money. If so, a dollar sign precedes the number.

TRUE	The value is money.
FALSE	The value is not money.

Parameter: `iDecimalPlaces`

Type: `int`

Description: The number of decimal places to be displayed.

Return value: The return value is a pointer to the resulting string (`szBuffer`).

FloatGetDlgItemRange

The `FloatGetDlgItemRange` function retrieves the valid range of a float control.

Syntax: `BOOL  FloatGetDlgItemRange(hDlg,iID,lpMin,lpMax)`

Parameter: `hDlg`

Type: `HWND`

Description: The window handle of the dialog box.

Parameter: `iID`

Type: `int`

Description: The control ID of the `tbFloat` control.

Parameter: `lpMin`

Type: `LPDOUBLE`

Description: Points to the variable that receives the minimum value for the control.

Parameter: `lpMax`

Type: `LPDOUBLE`

Description: Points to the variable that receives the maximum value for the control.

Return value: The return value is TRUE if the range is retrieved successfully; FALSE usually indicates the specified control isn't a float control.

Comments: This function is defined as a macro in powerpak.h.

FloatGetDlgItemValue

The `FloatGetDlgItemValue` function retrieves the current value of a float control represented as a double.

Syntax: `BOOL  FloatGetDlgItemValue(hDlg,iID,lpDouble)`

Parameter: `hDlg`

Type: `HWND`

Description: The window handle of the dialog box.

Parameter: `iID`

Type: `int`

Description: The control ID of the `tbFloat` control.

Parameter: `lpDouble`

Type: `LPDOUBLE`

Description: Pointer to a variable that receives the control's value.

Return value: The return value is TRUE if the value is retrieved successfully; FALSE usually indicates the specified control isn't a float control.

Comments: This function is defined as a macro in powerpak.h.

FloatGetFormat

The `FloatGetFormat` function gets the current format of a float control.

Syntax: `BOOL  FloatGetFormat(hWndFloat,lpFormat)`

Parameter: `hWndFloat`

Type: `HWND`

Description: The window handle of the `tbFloat` control.

Parameter: `lpFormat`

Type: `LPFLOATFORMAT`

Description: Points to a structure that contains the format parameters for the control.

Return value: The return value is TRUE if the format is retrieved successfully; FALSE usually indicates the specified control isn't a float control.

FloatGetRange

The `FloatGetRange` function retrieves the valid range of a float control.

Syntax: `BOOL  FloatGetRange(hWndFloat,lpMin,lpMax)`

Parameter: `hWndFloat`

Type: `HWND`

Description: The window handle of the `tbFloat` control.

Parameter: `lpMin`

Type: `LPDOUBLE`

Description: A pointer to a variable that receives the minimum value of the control.

Parameter: `lpMax`

Type: `LPDOUBLE`

Description: A pointer to a variable that receives the maximum value of the control.

Return value: The return value is TRUE if the range is retrieved successfully; FALSE usually indicates the specified control isn't a float control.

FloatGetValue

The `FloatGetValue` function retrieves the current value of a float control.

Syntax: `BOOL FloatGetValue(hWndFloat,lpDouble)`

Parameter: `hWndFloat`

Type: `HWND`

Description: The window handle of the `tbFloat` control.

Parameter: `lpDouble`

Type: `LPDOUBLE`

Description: A pointer to a variable that receives the value of the control.

Return value: The return value is TRUE if the value is retrieved successfully; FALSE usually indicates the specified control isn't a float control.

FloatSetDlgItemRange

The `FloatSetDlgItemRange` function sets the valid range of a float control.

Syntax: `BOOL FloatSetDlgItemRange(hDlg,iID,dfMin,dfMax)`

Parameter: `hDlg`

Type: `HWND`

Description: The window handle of the dialog box.

Parameter: `iID`

Type: `int`

Description: The control ID of the `tbFloat` control.

Parameter: `dfMin`

Type: `double`

Description: The minimum value for the control.

Parameter: `dfMax`

Type: `double`

Description: The maximum value for the control.

Return value: The return value is TRUE if the range is set successfully; FALSE usually indicates the specified control isn't a float control.

Comments: This function is defined as a macro in powerpak.h.

FloatSetDlgItemValue

The `FloatSetDlgItemValue` function sets the current value of a float control.

Syntax: `BOOL  FloatSetDlgItemValue(hDlg,iID,dfDouble)`

Parameter: `hDlg`

Type: `HWND`

Description: The window handle of the dialog box.

Parameter: `iID`

Type: `int`

Description: The control ID of the `tbFloat` control.

Parameter: `dfDouble`

Type: `double`

Description: The value to which the control is set.

Return value: The return value is TRUE if the value is set successfully; FALSE usually indicates the specified control isn't a float control.

Comments: This function is defined as a macro in powerpak.h.

FLOATSETFORMAT

The `FloatSetFormat` function sets the current format of a float control.

Syntax: `BOOL  FloatSetFormat(hWndFloat,lpFormat)`

Parameter: `hWndFloat`

Type: `HWND`

Description: The window handle of the `tbFloat` control.

Parameter: `lpFormat`

Type: `LPFLOATFORMAT`

Description: Points to a structure that contains the format parameters for the control.

Return value: The return value is TRUE if the format is set successfully; FALSE usually indicates the specified control isn't a float control.

FLOATSETMASK

The `FloatSetMask` function sets the current mask of a float control. This mask determines the number of characters the control accepts to the left and right of the decimal.

Syntax: `BOOL  FloatSetMask(hWndFloat,szMask)`

Parameter: `hWndFloat`

Type: `HWND`

Description: The window handle of the `tbFloat` control.

Parameter: `szMask`

Type: `LPSTR`

Description: A pointer to a string that contains the mask.

Return value: The return value is TRUE if the mask is set successfully; FALSE usually indicates the specified control isn't a float control.

Comments: The mask is defined as a series of nines fixing the maximum number of characters in the field. A decimal point must be placed in the field at the proper location.

Example: If you want the float field to display five characters to the left and two to the right of the decimal point, define the mask as 99999.99.

FLOATSETRANGE

The `FloatSetRange` function sets the valid range of a float control.

Syntax: `BOOL FloatSetRange(hWndFloat,dfMin,dfMax)`

Parameter: `hWndFloat`

Type: `HWND`

Description: The window handle of the `tbFloat` control.

Parameter: `dfMin`

Type: `double`

Description: The minimum value for the control.

Parameter: `dfMax`

Type: `double`

Description: The maximum value for the control.

Return value: The return value is TRUE if the range is set successfully; FALSE usually indicates the specified control isn't a float control.

FLOATSETSTYLE

The `FloatSetStyle` function sets the current style of a float control.

Syntax: `BOOL FloatSetStyle(hWnd,lStyle)`

Parameter: `hWnd`

Type: `HWND`

Description: The window handle of the `tbFloat` control.

Parameter: `lStyle`

Type: `LONG`

Description: A value representing the desired style bits for the control.

Return value: The return value is TRUE if the style is set successfully; FALSE usually indicates the specified control isn't a float control.

FLOATSETVALUE

The `FloatSetValue` function sets the current value of a float control.

Syntax: `BOOL  FloatSetValue(hWnd,dfDouble)`

Parameter: `hWnd`

Type: `HWND`

Description: The window handle of the `tbFloat` control.

Parameter: `dfDouble`

Type: `double`

Description: The value to which the control is set.

Return value: The return value is TRUE if the value is set successfully; FALSE usually indicates the specified control isn't a float control.

FLOATTOESTRING

The `FloatToEString` function converts a floating-point number to a formatted string in scientific notation.

Syntax:
```
LPSTR FloatToEString(szBuff,dfValue,nDigit,
    lpDecPnt,lpSign)
```

Parameter: `szBuff`

Type: `LPSTR`

Description: Points to the string that receives the formatted number.

Parameter: `dfValue`

Type: `double`

Description: The value to be converted.

Parameter: `nDigit`

Type: `int`

Description: The total number of digits to display.

Parameter: `lpDecPnt`

Type: `LPINT`

Description: The position of the decimal point from the left.

Parameter: `lpSign`

Type: `LPINT`

Description: A pointer to a variable that is set to a nonzero value if `dfValue` is negative.

Return value: The return value is a pointer to the resulting string.

FloatToFString

The `FloatToFString` function converts a floating-point number to a formatted string.

Syntax:
```
LPSTR  FloatToFString(szBuff,dfValue,nDec,
    lpDecPnt,lpSign)
```

Parameter: `szBuff`

Type: `LPSTR`

Description: Points to the string that receives the formatted number.

Parameter: `dfValue`

Type: `double`

Description: The value to be converted.

Parameter: `nDec`

Type: `int`

Description: The total number of digits to display.

Parameter: `lpDecPnt`

Type: `LPINT`

Description: The position of the decimal point from the left.

Parameter: `lpSign`

Type: `LPINT`

Description: Pointer to a variable that is set to nonzero if `dfValue` is negative.

Return value: The return value is a pointer to the resulting string.

THE IMPRINT CONTROL (TBIMPRINT)

The `tbImprint` is a static text control that gives the user interface a three-dimensional (3-D) appearance. Use of the control is nearly identical to the Windows `Static` class, but different border styles can be specified to achieve the 3-D effect. You can use the imprint control in place of the standard Windows group box, allowing large sections of the screen a 3-D appearance.

The control consists of several parts:

- Text area: a rectangular area where the static text is displayed. Depending on the imprint style, this area appears to be either pushed into or popped out from its surroundings, which might be the screen background or (if one is specified) the imprint frame.

- Frame: an optional frame around the text area. Depending on the style, the frame appears to be either pushed into or popped out from the screen background.
- An optional extra border either inside or outside the control.
- A shadow around all items, giving the control its 3-D appearance.

Many options are available for this control, so the developer should experiment with different styles and colors to achieve the visual effect that best suits the application.

IMPRINT DIALOG STATEMENT

The following statement places an imprint control in the resource file:

```
CONTROL text, id, "tbImprint",  style, x, y, width, height
```

`text` String to display inside the imprint control.

`id` Integer value that specifies the unique resource ID (or constant).

`style` Integer value that contains any combination of standard `WS_` styles and the following imprint styles:

```
IS_CLEAR
IS_FRAME_IN
IS_FRAME_OUT
IS_GROUPBOX
IS_IMPRINT_IN
IS_IMPRINT_OUT
IS_INSIDEBORDER
IS_OUTSIDEBORDER
IS_TEXTBORDER
IS_TEXTBOTTOM
```

```
IS_TEXTCENTER
IS_TEXTLEFT
IS_TEXTRIGHT
IS_TEXTTOP
IS_TEXTVCENTER
```

These styles are described more fully in the following section.

`x,y` Integer values that specify the x and y coordinates in the top-left corner of the control. The horizontal units are 1/4 of the dialog base width unit; the vertical units are 1/8 of the dialog base height unit.

`width` Integer value that specifies the width of the control. The width unit is 1/4 of the dialog base width unit.

`height` Integer value that specifies the height of the control. The height unit is 1/8 of the dialog base height unit.

IMPRINT CONTROL STYLES

The following styles are valid for use with the imprint control:

`IS_CLEAR`	Clears the inside of the control when it is drawn.
`IS_FRAME_IN`	Adds an inside frame set into the screen. The inside frame gives the appearance of a button in the imprint frame.
`IS_FRAME_OUT`	Adds an inside frame projected out from the screen. The inside frame gives the appearance of a button in the imprint frame.

IS_GROUPBOX	Imprint appears and acts as a group box. The text appears on the top of the border.
IS_IMPRINT_IN	Imprint looks like a push button (pushed into the screen).
IS_IMPRINT_OUT	Imprint looks like a push button (pushed out).
IS_INSIDEBORDER	Adds a border inside the normal border. This subtly changes the 3-D appearance of the control.
IS_OUTSIDEBORDER	Adds a border outside the border. This subtly changes the 3-D appearance of the control.
IS_TEXTBORDER	Places the text in the top border of the control (default when the style is IS_GROUPBOX).
IS_TEXTBOTTOM	Justifies the text to the bottom of the text portion of the control.
IS_TEXTCENTER	Centers the text horizontally in the control.
IS_TEXTLEFT	Justifies the text to the left of the control.
IS_TEXTRIGHT	Justifies the text to the right of the control.
IS_TEXTTOP	Justifies the text to the top of the control.
IS_TEXTVCENTER	Centers the text vertically in the control.

IMPRINT CONTROL MESSAGES

The following messages allow the application to communicate with the imprint control:

`IM_GETCOLOR` retrieves a structure that contains the colors used when drawing the various parts of the imprint control.

`IM_GETFRAMESIZE` retrieves the width of the frame (in pixels).

`IM_GETLINECNT` retrieves the number of lines of text being displayed.

`IM_GETLINESIZE` retrieves the width of the lines used to draw the control (in pixels).

`IM_GETSHADOWSIZE` retrieves the width of the shadow placed around the imprint control (in pixels).

`IM_SETCOLOR` specifies a structure that contains the colors for use in drawing the various parts of the imprint control.

`IM_SETFRAMESIZE` sets the width of the control's frame (in pixels).

`IM_SETLINECNT` sets the number of lines to display in the control.

`IM_SETLINESIZE` sets the width of the lines used to draw the control.

`IM_SETSHADOWSIZE` sets the size of the shadow placed around the imprint control (in pixels).

IMPRINT CONTROL EXAMPLES

The following resource statement creates a `tbImprint` control containing the text, "Hello World."

```
CONTROL "Hello World", IDD_IMPRINT, "tbImprint",
   WS_CHILD ¦  IS_IMPRINT_OUT ¦ IS_TEXTTOP ¦
   IS_TEXTLEFT,30,30,80,45
```

THE INTEGER CONTROL (TBINTEGER)

The `tbinteger` control provides validated entry of integer values. The application specifies minimum and maximum acceptable values at runtime. This control locks out the entry of any character other than a number.

INTEGER DIALOG STATEMENT

The following statement places a `tbInteger` control in the resource file:

```
CONTROL mask, id, "tbinteger", style, x, y, width, height
```

`mask` String that specifies the size of the integer field. Specifically, the number of nines specified in this field denotes the total number of digits the user can enter. (See the Integer Control Examples section to follow.)

`id` Integer value that specifies the unique resource ID.

`style` Integer value that contains any combination of the standard `WS_` styles.

`x,y` Integer values that specify the x and y coordinates of the top-left corner of the control. The horizontal units are 1/4 of the dialog base width unit; the vertical units are 1/8 of the dialog base height unit.

`width` Integer value that specifies the width of the control. The width unit is 1/4 of the dialog base width unit.

`height` Integer value that specifies the height of the control. The height unit is 1/8 of the dialog base height unit.

INTEGER CONTROL STYLES

The following styles can be used with the float control:

`IS_SPIN`	Adds a spin button to the right side of the control so the user can change the value using the mouse.
`IS_SPINWRAP`	If `IS_SPIN` is specified, it causes the value to wrap alternately from maximum to minimum.

INTEGER CONTROL EXAMPLES

The following resource statement creates an integer control that accepts a number with five digits:

```
CONTROL "99999", "tbinteger", IDD_INTFIELD,
   WS_TABSTOP ¦ WS_BORDER ¦ WS_CHILD,
   10, 10, 100, 12
```

The following code then sets the range of the control from –10,000 to 10,000. This code typically is placed in the `WM_INITDIALOG` section of the dialog procedure.

```
IntSetDlgItemRange(hWnd, IDD_INTFIELD, -10000L, 10000L);
```

INTEGER CONTROL FUNCTIONS

The following API calls support the integer controls. The function prototypes for these functions are contained in powerpak.h. All functions are declared as `FAR` and `PASCAL`.

TABLE 2.4. INTEGER CONTROL FUNCTIONS.

Function	*Description*
`IntGetDlgItemRange`	Same as `IntGetRange`, but accepts dialog ID as parameter.
`IntGetDlgItemValue`	Same as `IntGetValue`, but accepts dialog ID as parameter.
`IntGetRange`	Retrieves the current minimum and maximum range for the control.
`IntGetValue`	Retrieves the value from the integer control.
`IntGetSpin`	Gets the parameters associated with the spin button.
`IntSetDlgItemRange`	Same as `IntSetRange`, but accepts dialog ID as parameter.
`IntSetDlgItemValue`	Same as `IntSetValue`, but accepts dialog ID as parameter.
`IntSetMask`	Sets the mask specifying the number of digits to be entered.
`IntSetRange`	Sets the minimum and maximum range for the control.
`IntSetSpin`	Sets the parameters associated with the spin button.
`IntSetValue`	Loads the specified value into the integer control.

INTGETDLGITEMRANGE

The `IntGetDlgItemRange` function retrieves the minimum and maximum range of an integer control.

Syntax: `BOOL  IntGetDlgItemRange(hDlg,iID,lpMin,lpMax)`

Parameter: `hDlg`

Type: `HWND`

Description: The window handle of the dialog box.

Parameter: `iID`

Type: `int`

Description: The control ID of the `tbInteger` control.

Parameter: `lpMin`

Type: `LPLONG`

Description: Points to a variable that receives the minimum value of the control.

Parameter: `lpMax`

Type: `LPLONG`

Description: Points to a variable that receives the maximum value of the control.

Return value: The return value is TRUE if the range is retrieved successfully; FALSE usually indicates the specified control isn't an integer control.

Comments: This function is defined as a macro in powerpak.h.

IntGetDlgItemValue

The `IntGetDlgItemValue` function retrieves the current value of an integer control.

Syntax: `BOOL  IntGetDlgItemValue(hDlg,iID,lpLong)`

Parameter: `hDlg`

Type: `HWND`

Description: The window handle of the dialog box.

Parameter: `iID`

Type: `int`

Description: The control ID of the `tbInteger` control.

Parameter: `lpLong`

Type: `LPLONG`

Description: Points to a variable that receives the control's value.

Return value: The return value is TRUE if the value is retrieved successfully; FALSE usually indicates the specified control isn't an integer control.

Comments: This function is defined as a macro in powerpak.h.

IntGetRange

The `IntGetRange` function retrieves the minimum and maximum range of an integer control.

Syntax: `BOOL  IntGetRange(hWndInt,lpMin,lpMax)`

Parameter: `hWndInt`

Type: `HWND`

Description: The window handle of the `tbInteger` control.

Parameter: `lpMin`

Type: `LPINT`

Description: Points to a variable that receives the control's minimum value.

Parameter: `lpMax`

Type: `LPINT`

Description: Points to a variable that receives the control's maximum value.

Return value: The return value is TRUE if the range is retrieved successfully; FALSE usually indicates the specified control isn't an integer control.

IntGetSpin

The `IntGetSpin` function determines whether a spin box has been added to the integer control and retrieves the current values.

Syntax: `BOOL IntGetSpin(hWndInt,lpfSpinWrap,lpfSpinInc)`

Parameter: `hWndInt`

Type: `HWND`

Description: The window handle of the `tbInteger` control.

Parameter: `lpfSpinWrap`

Type: `LPBOOL`

Description: The value returned determines whether the value wraps to the beginning or end upon reaching the maximum or minimum value.

Parameter: `lpfSpinInc`

Type: `LPLONG`

Description: The value returned determines the incremental value used.

Return value: The return value is TRUE if the integer control currently shows a spin button; if not, the value is FALSE.

IntGetValue

The `IntGetValue` function retrieves the current value of an integer control.

Syntax: `BOOL IntGetValue(hWndInt,lpLong)`

Parameter: `hWndInt`

Type: `HWND`

Description: The window handle of the `tbInteger` control.

Parameter: `lpLong`

Type: `LPLONG`

Description: Points to a variable that receives the control's minimum value.

Return value: The return value is TRUE if the range is retrieved successfully; FALSE usually indicates the specified control isn't an integer control.

IntSetDlgItemRange

The `IntSetDlgItemRange` function sets the minimum and maximum values of an integer control.

Syntax: `BOOL IntSetDlgItemRange(hDlg,iID,lMin,lMax)`

Parameter: `hDlg`

Type: `HWND`

Description: The window handle of the dialog box.

Parameter: `iID`

Type: `int`

Description: The control ID of the `tbInteger` control.

Parameter: `lMin`

Type: `LONG`

Description: The minimum value for the control.

Parameter: `lMax`

Type: `LONG`

Description: The maximum value for the control.

Return value: The return value is TRUE if the range is set successfully; FALSE usually indicates the specified control isn't an integer control.

Comments: This function is defined as a macro in powerpak.h.

IntSetDlgItemValue

The `IntSetDlgItemValue` function sets the current value of an integer control.

Syntax: `BOOL IntSetDlgItemValue(hDlg,iID,lValue)`

Parameter: `hDlg`

Type: `HWND`

Description: The window handle of the dialog box.

Parameter: `iID`

Type: `int`

Description: The control ID of the `tbInteger` control.

Parameter: `lValue`

Type: `LONG`

Description: The value for the control.

Return value: The return value is TRUE if the value is set successfully; FALSE usually indicates the specified control isn't an integer control.

Comments: This function is defined as a macro in powerpak.h.

IntSetMask

The `IntSetMask` function sets the mask for the integer control.

Syntax: `BOOL IntSetMask(hWndInt,szMask)`

Parameter: `hWndInt`

Type: `HWND`

Description: The window handle of the `tbInteger` control.

Parameter: `szMask`

Type: `LPSTR`

Description: The mask to be used.

Return value: The return value is TRUE if the mask is set successfully; FALSE usually indicates the specified control isn't an integer control.

IntSetRange

The `IntSetRange` function sets the minimum and maximum value of an integer control.

Syntax: `BOOL IntSetRange(hWndInt,lMin,lMax)`

Parameter: `hWndInt`

Type: `HWND`

Description: The window handle of the `tbInteger` control.

Parameter: `lMin`

Type: `LONG`

Description: The minimum value for the control.

Parameter: `lMax`

Type: `LONG`

Description: The maximum value for the control.

Return value: The return value is TRUE if the range is set successfully; FALSE usually indicates the specified control isn't an integer control.

IntSetSpin

The `IntSetSpin` function displays or hides the spin box and sets the spin box parameters.

Syntax: `BOOL IntSetSpin(hWndInt,fSpin, fSpinWrap, fSpinInc)`

Parameter: `hWndInt`

Type: `HWND`

Description: The window handle of the `tbInteger` control.

Parameter: `fSpin`

Type: `BOOL`

Description: This value determines whether the spin button should be displayed or hidden.

Parameter: `fSpinWrap`

Type: `BOOL`

Description: This value determines whether the value wraps to the beginning or end upon reaching the maximum or minimum value.

Parameter: `fSpinInc`

Type: `LONG`

Description: This value specifies the incremental value in use.

Return value: The return value is TRUE if the operation is successful, FALSE if it isn't.

IntSetValue

The `IntSetValue` function sets the current value of an integer control.

Syntax: `BOOL   IntSetValue(hWndInt,iValue)`

Parameter: `hWndInt`

Type: `HWND`

Description: The window handle of the `tbInteger` control.

Parameter: `iValue`

Type: `int`

Description: The value for the control.

Return value: The return value is TRUE if the value is set successfully; FALSE usually indicates the specified control isn't an integer control.

IntToString

The `IntToString` function converts an integer to a string.

Syntax: `LPSTR  IntToString(iValue,szString)`

Parameter: `iValue`

Type: `int`

Description: The value to be converted.

Parameter: `szString`

Type: `LPSTR`

Description: Points to a string that receives the formatted number.

Return value: The return value is a pointer to the resulting string (`szString`).

The Progress Control (tbProgress)

The `tbProgress` control displays a graphical indication of the progress of an operation. The application program sends messages to the control, which displays the filled progress bar and, optionally, the percentage completed.

The application program sets a minimum and maximum range for the progress bar (normally from zero to a predetermined upper limit) and periodically sends messages to the control indicating the current value, which must be within the range. The control automatically displays the appropriate length progress bar and, if required, displays the percentage completed.

Progress Dialog Statement

The following statement places a `tbProgress` control in the resource file:

```
CONTROL "", id, "tbProgress",  style, x, y, width, height
```

`id` Integer value that specifies the unique resource ID.

`style` Integer value that contains any combination of the standard `WS_` styles and the following Progress styles:

`PS_HIDEPERCENTAGE`
`PS_HORIZONTAL`
`PS_VERTICAL`

These styles are described more fully in the next section.

`x,y` Integer values that specify the x and y coordinates of the top-left corner of the control. The horizontal units are 1/4 of the dialog base width unit; the vertical units are 1/8 of the dialog base height unit.

`width` Integer value that specifies the width of the control. The width unit is 1/4 of the dialog base width unit.

`height` Integer value that specifies the height of the control. The height unit is 1/8 of the dialog base height unit.

PROGRESS CONTROL STYLES

The following styles are valid for a `tbProgress` control:

`PS_VERTICAL` specifies that the progress bar be displayed vertically. The bar begins filling from the bottom and proceeds to the top. This is the default.

`PS_HORIZONTAL` specifies that the progress bar be displayed horizontally. The bar begins filling from the left and proceeds to the right.

PS_HIDEPERCENTAGE by default, the tbProgress control calculates the percentage complete and displays it in the center of the control. This style suppresses the percent display.

Progress Control Messages

The following messages permit the application to communicate with the tbProgress control:

PM_SETRANGE sets the range of the progress control (the default range is 0 to 100).

PM_GETRANGE retrieves the current range of the progress control.

PM_SETPOS sets the current value of the progress bar.

PM_GETPOS retrieves the current value of the progress bar.

Progress Control Examples

The following resource statement defines a horizontal progress bar:

```
CONTROL "", IDD_PROGRESS, "tbProgress",
   WS_CHILD ¦ WS_BORDER ¦ PS_HORIZONTAL,
   8, 20, 80, 12
```

In the code that processes the WM_INITDIALOG (or WM_CREATE) message for the control's dialog, the following sets the range from 0 to 1,000.

```
SendDlgItemMessage(hWnd, IDD_PROGRESS, PM_SETRANGE,
                   NULL, MAKELONG(0, 1000));
```

To set the progress control to mid-range:

```
SendDlgItemMessage(hWnd, IDD_PROGRESS, PM_SETPOS, 500,
                   NULL);
```

THE SPINBUTTON CONTROL (TBSPINBUTTON)

The `tbSpinButton` control consists of two arrows aligned either horizontally or vertically. It is used as a replacement for traditional scroll bars when only the arrows are required and not the bar between.

The `tbSpinButton` control sends a `WM_HSCROLL` and `WM_VSCROLL` message to its parent.

SPINBUTTON DIALOG STATEMENT

The following statement places a `tbSpinButton` control in the resource file:

```
CONTROL "", id, "tbSpinButton",  style, x, y, width,
    height
```

`id` Integer value that specifies the unique resource ID.

`style` Integer value that contains any combination of the standard `WS_` styles and the following `tbSpinButton` styles:

```
SBNS_DOWNARROW
SBNS_HORIZONTAL
SBNS_UPARROW
SBNS_UPDOWNARROW
SBNS_VERTICAL
```

These styles are described more fully in the next section.

`x,y` Integer values that specify the x and y coordinates of the top-left corner of the control. The horizontal units are 1/4 of the dialog base width unit; the vertical units are 1/8 of the dialog base height unit.

`width` Integer value that specifies the width of the control. The width unit is 1/4 of the dialog base width unit.

`height` Integer value that specifies the height of the control. The height unit is 1/8 of the dialog base height unit.

SpinButton Control Styles

The following styles are valid for use with the `tbSpinButton` control:

`SBNS_DOWNARROW` specifies that the control consist of a down arrow only. By default, both up and down arrows are displayed.

`SBNS_HORIZONTAL` specifies that the control arrows are aligned horizontally.

`SBNS_UPARROW` specifies that the control consist of an up arrow only. By default, both up and down arrows are displayed.

`SBNS_UPDOWNARROW` specifies that both up and down arrows are displayed. This is the default style.

`SBNS_VERTICAL` specifies that the control arrows are vertically stacked. This is the default style.

SpinButton Control Example

The following resource statement creates a horizontally aligned `tbSpinButton` control:

```
CONTROL "", IDD_SPIN, "tbSpinButton",
   WS_CHILD ¦ WS_BORDER ¦ SBNS_HORIZONTAL,
   30, 30, 30, 12
```

THE TIME CONTROL (TBTIME)

tbTime is a formatted time control supporting several common formats. The character that separates the hours, minutes, and seconds (: in the following example) is determined from the Windows setup.

The tbTime control performs data validation when the control loses focus, not on each keystroke. The parent receives an EN_INVALIDDATA message if the control contains an invalid time. In this case, the parent must determine the proper course of action, but usually the time field clears and gives the user another chance.

You must use the standard SetDlgItemText and GetDlgItemText API calls (or the WM_GETTEXT and WM_SETTEXT messages) to set or retrieve the time from the control.

TIME DIALOG STATEMENT

The following statement places a tbTime control in the resource file:

```
CONTROL "", id, "tbTime",  style, x, y, width, height
```

id — Integer value that specifies the unique resource ID.

style — Integer value that contains any combination of the standard WS_ styles and the following tbTime styles:

TS_12HOUR
TS_24HOUR
TS_SECONDS

These styles are described more fully in the next section.

x,y — Integer values that specify the x and y coordinates of the top-left corner of the control. The horizontal units are 1/4 of the dialog base width unit; the vertical units are 1/8 of the dialog base height unit.

`width` Integer value that specifies the width of the control. The width unit is 1/4 of the dialog base width unit.

`height` Integer value that specifies the height of the control. The height unit is 1/8 of the dialog base height unit.

Time Control Styles

The following styles are valid for use with the `tbTime` control:

`TS_12HOUR` The time is entered and displayed in 12-hour format with an AM or PM designator. (This is the default style.)

`TS_24HOUR` The time is entered and displayed in 24-hour format.

`TS_SECONDS` The time includes seconds. The default is to display only hours and minutes.

Time Control Example

The following resource statement creates a `tbTime` control with a 12-hour display. Seconds are displayed.

```
CONTROL "", IDD_TIME, "tbTime",
   WS_CHILD | WS_BORDER | TS_12HOUR | TS_SECONDS,
   30, 30, 50, 12
```

Time Control Related Functions

The following functions are not needed to effectively use the `tbTime` control, but they can be useful when manipulating the times already entered.

TABLE 2.5. TIME CONTROL FUNCTIONS.

Function	*Description*
`TimeGetCurrentTime`	Gets the current time as a string in the specified format.
`TimeGetDlgItemFormat`	Retrieves the format of the time control (dialog version).
`TimeGetFormat`	Retrieves the format of the time control (child window version).
`TimeHMSToSeconds`	Converts an hour, minute, and second to the total number of seconds.
`TimeHMSToString`	Converts an hour, minute, and second to a time string.
`TimeSecondsToHMS`	Converts a number of seconds to hour, minute, and second.
`TimeSetDlgItemFormat`	Sets the format of the time control (dialog version).
`TimeSetDlgItemRange`	Specifies a range of valid times (dialog version).
`TimeSetFormat`	Sets the format of the time control (child window version).
`TimeSetRange`	Specifies a range of valid times.
`TimeStringIsValid`	Determines whether a time string is valid.
`TimeStringToHMS`	Converts a time string to hour, minute, and second.

TIMEGETCURRENTTIME

The `TimeGetCurrentTime` function retrieves the current time in the specified format.

Syntax: `void TimeGetCurrentTime(lpszTime,lpTimeFormat)`

Parameter: `lpszTime`

Type: `LPSTR`

Description: The string to receive the current time.

Parameter: `lpTimeFormat`

Type: `LPTIMEFORMAT`

Description: Points to a structure that contains the formatting parameters.

Return value: None.

TimeGetDlgItemFormat

The `TimeGetDlgItemFormat` function retrieves the display format of a time control.

Syntax: `BOOL  TimeGetDlgItemFormat(hDlg,iID,lpTimeFormat)`

Parameter: `hDlg`

Type: `HWND`

Description: The window handle of the dialog box.

Parameter: `iID`

Type: `int`

Description: The control ID of the `tbTime` control.

Parameter: `lpTimeFormat`

Type: `LPTIMEFORMAT`

Description: Points to a structure that contains the formatting parameters.

Return value: The return value is TRUE if the format is retrieved.

Comments: This function is defined as a macro in powerpak.h.

TimeGetFormat

The `TimeGetFormat` function retrieves the display format of a time control.

Syntax: `BOOL  TimeGetFormat(hWndTime,lpTimeFormat)`

Parameter: `hWndTime`

Type: `HWND`

Description: The window handle of the `tbTime` control.

Parameter: `lpTimeFormat`

Type: `LPTIMEFORMAT`

Description: Pointer to a structure that contains the formatting parameters.

Return value: The return value is TRUE if the format is retrieved.

TimeHMSToSeconds

The `TimeHMSToSeconds` function converts the hour/minute/second format to the number of seconds since midnight.

Syntax: `LONG  TimeHMSToSeconds(lpTime)`

Parameter: `lpTime`

Type: `LPTIME`

Description: Pointer to the structure that contains the hour, minute, and second.

Return value: The return value is the number of seconds in the hour, minute, and second.

TimeHMSToString

The `TimeHMSToString` function converts an hour/minute/second time to a string in the specified format.

Syntax: `LPSTR TimeHMSToString(lpTime,lpszStr,lpTimeFormat)`

Parameter: `lpTime`

Type: `LPTIME`

Description: Pointer to the structure that contains the hour, minute, and second.

Parameter: `lpszStr`

Type: `LPSTR`

Description: Points to a string that contains the formatted time.

Parameter: `lpTimeFormat`

Type: `LPTIMEFORMAT`

Description: Pointer to a structure that defines the formatting parameter to be used.

Return value: The return value is a pointer to the string containing the time.

TimeSecondsToHMS

The `TimeSecondsToHMS` function converts the number of seconds since midnight to the hour/minute/second structure.

Syntax: `LPTIME  TimeSecondsToHMS(lSeconds,lpTime)`

Parameter: `lSeconds`

Type: `LONG`

Description: The number of seconds elapsed since midnight.

Parameter: `lpTime`

Type: `LPTIME`

Description: Pointer to the structure that contains the hour, minute, and second.

Return value: The return value is a pointer to the `lpTime` structure.

TimeSetDlgItemFormat

The `TimeSetDlgItemFormat` function sets the display format of a time control.

Syntax: `BOOL  TimeSetDlgItemFormat(hDlg,iID,lpTimeFormat)`

Parameter: `hDlg`

Type: `HWND`

Description: The window handle of the dialog box.

Parameter: `iID`

Type: `int`

Description: The control ID of the `tbTime` control.

Parameter: `lpTimeFormat`

Type: `LPTIMEFORMAT`

Description: Pointer to a structure that contains the formatting parameters.

Return value: The function returns TRUE if the format is set successfully.

Comments: This function is defined as a macro in powerpak.h.

TimeSetDlgItemRange

The `TimeSetDlgItemRange` function sets the valid range of a time control.

Syntax: `BOOL  TimeSetDlgItemRange(hDlg,iID, lpTimeStart, lpTimeEnd)`

Parameter: `hDlg`

Type: `HWND`

Description: The window handle of the dialog box.

Parameter: `iID`

Type: `int`

Description: The control ID of the `tbTime` control.

Parameter: `lpTimeStart`

Type: `LPTIME`

Description: Pointer to a structure that contains the earliest valid time.

Parameter: `lpTimeEnd`

Type: `LPTIME`

Description: Pointer to a structure that contains the latest valid time.

Return value: The return value is TRUE if the range is set successfully.

Comments: This function is defined as a macro in powerpak.h.

TIMESETFORMAT

The `TimeSetFormat` function sets the display format of a time control.

Syntax: `BOOL  TimeSetFormat(hWndTime,lpTimeFormat)`

Parameter: `hWndTime`

Type: `HWND`

Description: The window handle of the `tbTime` control.

Parameter: `lpTimeFormat`

Type: `LPTIMEFORMAT`

Description: Pointer to a structure that contains the formatting parameters.

Return value: The function returns TRUE if the format is set successfully.

TimeSetRange

The `TimeSetRange` function sets the valid range of a time control.

Syntax: `BOOL TimeSetRange(hWndTime,lpTimeStart,lpTimeEnd)`

Parameter: `hWndTime`

Type: `HWND`

Description: The window handle of the `tbTime` control.

Parameter: `lpTimeStart`

Type: `LPTIME`

Description: Pointer to a structure that contains the earliest valid time.

Parameter: `lpTimeEnd`

Type: `LPTIME`

Description: Pointer to a structure that contains the latest valid time.

Return value: The return value is TRUE if the range is set successfully.

TimeStringIsValid

The `TimeStringIsValid` function returns TRUE if the specified string contains a valid time.

Syntax: `BOOL  TimeStringIsValid(lpszTime,lpTimeFormat)`

Parameter: `lpszTime`

Type: `LPSTR`

Description: Points to a string that contains the time string.

Parameter: `lpTimeFormat`

Type: `LPTIMEFORMAT`

Description: Points to a structure that contains the formatting parameters to which the string must conform.

Return value: The return value is TRUE if the string contains a valid time, FALSE if it doesn't.

TIMESTRINGTOHMS

The `TimeStringToHMS` function converts a string time (12:45:33) to an hour/minute/second structure.

Syntax: `LPTIME  TimeStringToHMS(lpszTimeString,lpTime, lpTimeFormat)`

Parameter: `lpszTimeString`

Type: `LPSTR`

Description: Points to a string that contains the time.

Parameter: `lpTime`

Type: `LPTIME`

Description: Points to a structure that receives the hour, minute, and second values.

Parameter: `lpTimeFormat`

Type: `LPTIMEFORMAT`

Description: Points to a structure that defines the formatting parameters to which the string must conform.

Return value: The return value is a pointer to the `lpTime` structure.

THE VIEWTEXT CONTROL (TBVIEWTEXT)

The `tbViewText` control provides a versatile method of displaying a variably-sized block of text. This control can be described as a multi-line static text field, but it has sophisticated column and row locking capabilities and doesn't require that the entire text remain in memory at once. The features of the `tbViewText` control make it perfect for displaying financial or other tabular data. It is also quite useful for displaying README or other text files.

A `tbViewText` control consists of the following distinct sections. Notice that not all these sections apply to every application of the control:

- The *main header* occupies one or more lines at the top of the text. If a main header is specified, it always remains at the top of the control and doesn't scroll in either direction.
- The *column header*, which occupies one or more lines, usually defines the meaning of data in the columns beneath it. If a column header is specified, it too remains at the top of the control (under the main header if one exists). Unlike the main header, the column header scrolls left and right if there is more data than can fit across the window.
- The *row header*, which occupies one or more columns, usually defines the meaning of data in the row to the right of the header. If a row header is specified, it remains at the left side of the control at all times. This section of the control scrolls up and down if there is more data than can fit across the window.
- The *text area* is the only section that is present in every `tbViewText` control. It contains at least one line of text.
- The *scroll bars* automatically appear if there is more data (horizontally or vertically) than can be displayed in the current control window size.

Various foreground and background colors can be specified for each of these sections. Because the control was originally developed to display tabular information, it currently supports only nonproportional fonts.

VIEWTEXT DIALOG STATEMENT

The following statement places a `tbViewText` control in the resource file:

```
CONTROL "", id, "tbViewText", style, x, y, width, height
```

`id` Integer value that specifies the unique resource ID.

`style` Integer value that contains any combination of the standard `WS_` styles and the following `FileList` styles:

```
VTS_NOHSCROLLBAR
VTS_NOVSCROLLBAR
VTS_OWNERSUPPLYTEXT
```

These styles are described more fully in the next section.

`x,y` Integer values that specify the x and y coordinates of the top-left corner of the control. The horizontal units are 1/4 of the dialog base width unit; the vertical units are 1/8 of the dialog base height unit.

`width` Integer value that specifies the width of the control. The width unit is 1/4 of the dialog base width unit.

`height` Integer value that specifies the height of the control. The height unit is 1/8 of the dialog base height unit.

Note: The actual text to display isn't specified in the resource statement. You must load the desired text into the control at runtime using the facilities described in the following sections.

VIEWTEXT CONTROL STYLES

The following styles are legal with the `tbViewText` control:

VTS_NOHSCROLLBAR	This style indicates that no horizontal scroll bar be displayed. If the text size is greater than the control window, the user must use the keyboard to see the excess.
VTS_NOVSCROLLBAR	This style indicates that no vertical scroll bar be displayed. If the text size is greater than the control window, the user must use the keyboard to see the excess.
VTS_OWNERSUPPLYTEXT	This style indicates that the control will store only as much text as it can currently display. When additional lines are needed, it requests them through the VTM_RETRIEVETEXT message. By using this style, you can display a large document and keep memory requirements to a minimum, retrieving text from the file as needed.

VIEWTEXT CONTROL MESSAGES

The following messages allow the application to communicate with the `tbViewText` control:

VTM_ADDSTRING adds a line to the bottom of the text.

VTM_CLEAR removes all text from the control.

VTM_DELETESTRING deletes the specified line from the text.

VTM_GETCOLOR retrieves a structure that contains the current colors for all sections of the control.

VTM_GETLINECOUNT returns the current number of text lines.

VTM_GETSTRING retrieves one of the lines from the text.

VTM_GETSTRINGLEN retrieves the length of a text line.

VTM_GETTOPINDEX returns the number of the line currently at the top of the display.

VTM_HIGHLIGHTTEXT highlights a portion of the text.

VTM_INSERTSTRING inserts a line in the middle of existing text.

VTM_REDRAW causes an immediate redraw of the control.

VTM_SEARCH searches for the first occurrence of the key string in the text. If found, the appropriate line scrolls to the top of the display, and the text is highlighted.

VTM_SEARCHREPEAT repeats the last search, beginning immediately after the last encountered match. If another match is found, the appropriate line scrolls to the top of the display, and the text is highlighted.

VTM_SETCOLHEADERS specifies the number of characters from the left of the text that are locked as a column header. (The default is zero.)

VTM_SETCOLOR specifies a structure that contains the colors for all sections of the control.

VTM_SETHEADER specifies the number of lines at the top of the text to be used by the main header. (The default is zero.)

VTM_SETROWHEADERS specifies the number of lines occupied by the row header. (If there is a main header, the row header is assumed to begin at the following line.)

VTM_SETTOPINDEX specifies the first line of the display. That line immediately scrolls to the top.

VTM_RETRIEVETEXT is sent to the control's parent when the control requires more text to display. This message is used when the style is VTS_OWNERSUPPLYTEXT.

VTM_VIEWSIZE is sent to the control's parent if the style is VTS_OWNERSUPPLYTEXT. The parent must specify the maximum width and number of lines.

VIEWTEXT CONTROL EXAMPLE

The following resource statement creates a standard tbViewText control:

```
CONTROL "", IDD_VIEWTEXT, "tbViewText", WS_CHILD ¦
    WS_TABSTOP, 30, 30, 100, 100
```

The following code, which would probably occur in the WM_INITDIALOG (or WM_CREATE) section of the control's window procedure, reads a file and sends the text to the control.

```
SendDlgItemMessage(hWnd, IDD_VIEWTEXT, VTM_CLEAR,
                   NULL, NULL);
f1 = fopen("textfile", "r");
do
   {
   fgets(f1, Buffer, 80);  // read the next line
   if (!feof(f1))
      SendDlgItemMessage(hWnd, IDD_VIEWTEXT,
                         VTM_ADDSTRING,
                         NULL, (LONG)(LPSTR)Buffer);
   } while (!feof(f1));

fclose(f1);
```

THE VIEWPICT CONTROL (TBVIEWPICT)

The `tbViewPict` control provides a simple yet versatile method for displaying graphics images. The control supports three picture formats (BMP, PCX, and GIF) and automatically sizes the bitmap to the destination area. Alternately, it displays portions of the bitmap and permits scrolling. The control also supports timer-driven frame animation of bitmap images.

VIEWPICT DIALOG STATEMENT

The following statement places a `tbViewPict` control in the resource file:

```
CONTROL name, id, "tbViewPict",  style, x, y, width, height
```

`name` A string that defines the resource name or filename of the bitmap.

`id` The integer value that specifies the unique resource ID.

`style` The integer value that contains any combination of the standard `WS_` styles and the following `ViewPict` styles:

```
VPS_BMP
VPS_CENTER
VPS_FREEZE
VPS_GIF
VPS_MAINTAINSCALE
VPS_NORMAL
VPS_PCX
VPS_RESOURCE
VPS_SCROLL
```

VPS_SHOWFRAMEONCE
VPS_STATIC
VPS_STRETCH

These styles are described more fully in the next section.

`x,y`	Integer values that specify the x and y coordinates of the top-left corner of the control. The horizontal units are 1/4 of the dialog base width unit; the vertical units are 1/8 of the dialog base height unit.
`width`	Integer value that specifies the width of the control. The width unit is 1/4 of the dialog base width unit.
`height`	Integer value that specifies the height of the control. The height unit is 1/8 of the dialog base height unit.

ViewPict Control Styles

The following styles are valid for `tbViewPict` controls:

`VPS_BMP`	Specifies that the picture is in Windows BMP format.
`VPS_CENTER`	The bitmap is to be centered in the control window.
`VPS_FREEZE`	If the control is animated, this specifies that the animation is initially frozen. It must be started by the application through the `VPM_STARTANIMATION` message.
`VPS_GIF`	Specifies that the picture is in CompuServe's GIF format.

VPS_MAINTAINSCALE	Valid with VPS_STRETCH, this style indicates that the original scale of the bitmap is retained. The control uses a best fit algorithm to determine how to display the bitmap in original scale while using as much of the control window as possible.
VPS_NORMAL	Specifies that the bitmap be displayed in its original dimensions, regardless of the size of the control. If the bitmap is larger than the control window, the top-left portion of the bitmap is displayed. If VPS_SCROLL (the default style) is set, scroll bars enable viewing the rest of the image.
VPS_PCX	Specifies that the picture is in PCX format.
VPS_RESOURCE	Specifies that the bitmap is stored in the resource file (must be type VIEWPICT). The default assumes that the bitmap is in a file.
VPS_SCROLL	If the bitmap is larger than the control window, this style adds scroll bars to permit the rest of the bitmap to be viewed.
VPS_SHOWFRAMEONCE	When assigning a frame for animation, this style can be used to specify that the frame be shown only once.

`VPS_STATIC`	Specifies that the picture control is static. This is useful for background images because the control never receives input focus. It remains in the background at all times.
`VPS_STRETCH`	The bitmap is stretched or compressed to fit the exact dimensions of the control window.

VIEWPICT CONTROL MESSAGES

The following messages allow the application to communicate with the `tbViewPict` control:

`VPM_CLEAR`	Clears the control to the background color.
`VPM_FREEZEANIMATION`	Halts the animation at the current frame.
`VPM_SETFRAMES`	Specifies a structure that defines frames and other information used for animation.
`VPM_SETPICTURE`	Changes the picture associated with the control.
`VPM_SETSTYLE`	Sets or changes the style bits of the control.

VPM_SHOWNEXTFRAME	Displays the next frame in the series. This is valid only if the automatic animation is frozen. When the last frame is reached, the control wraps around to the first frame.
VPM_SHOWPREVFRAME	Displays the previous frame in the series. This is valid only if the automatic animation is frozen. When the first frame is reached, the control wraps around to the last frame.
VPM_STARTANIMATION	Starts up the animation at the point it was frozen.
VPN_KILLFOCUS	This message is sent to the parent as part of WM_COMMAND when the control loses focus.
VPN_SETFOCUS	This message is sent to the parent as part of WM_COMMAND when the control gains focus.
WM_CTLCOLOR	Sent to the parent to determine the background color used as a filler around the picture.

ViewPict Control Example

The following statement in the resource file defines the mylogo.pcx file as a resource object of type `VIEWPICT`:

```
Logo  VIEWPICT mylogo.pcx
```

The following resource statement creates a `tbViewPict` control that displays the preceding bitmap:

```
CONTROL "Logo", IDD_LOGO, "tbViewPict",
    WS_CHILD ¦ WS_TABSTOP ¦ VPS_STRETCH ¦ VPS_PCX
    VPS_RESOURCE, 0, 0, 100, 100
```

3

PowerPack Functions

This chapter contains information on the general functions supplied by the PowerPack DLL. The functions are grouped logically according to type. A program using any of these functions must include powerpak.h and link with POWERPAK.LIB, the import library for the DLL, which contains these functions.

File I/O Functions

As a general rule, you shouldn't use buffered file I/O in Windows programs. Instead, to open a file, use the SDK `_lopen` function, which returns an MS-DOS file handle. The following PowerPack functions provide enhanced file support using the file handle returned by the `_lopen` call. All the functions that read or write data to a file accept far pointers by default, making them more useful than the corresponding C runtime calls.

TABLE 3.1. FILE I/O FUNCTIONS.

Function	*Description*
`ErrorNo`	Returns the error code from the last PowerPack file operation.
`FileClose`	Closes a file.
`FileExists`	Determines if specified file exists on the drive.
`FileFindFirst`	Finds first matching file in a directory.
`FileFindNext`	Finds next matching file in a directory.
`FileGetc`	Reads one character from the file.
`FileGetDateTime`	Gets a file's date/time stamp.
`FileGetf`	Reads one floating-point value from the file.
`FileGetl`	Reads one long integer from the file.
`FileGets`	Reads one string from the file.
`FileGetw`	Reads one 16-bit word from the file.
`FileOpen`	Opens a file.
`FilePutc`	Writes one character to the file.
`FilePutf`	Writes one floating-point value to the file.

Function	*Description*
`FilePutl`	Writes one long integer to the file.
`FilePuts`	Writes one string to the file.
`FilePutw`	Writes one 16-bit word to the file.
`FileRead`	Reads block of data from the file (similar to `fread`).
`FileRemove`	Deletes a file.
`FileSeek`	Moves to a specified position in the file.
`FileSetDateTime`	Sets a file's date/time stamp.
`FileWrite`	Writes block of data to the file.

The following are higher level file functions:

Parameter: `FileCopy`

Description: Automatically copies a single file to a new filename.

Parameter: `FileMultipleCopy`

Description: Copies multiple files (using wildcards).

ErrorNo

The `ErrorNo` function returns the error code from the last PowerPack file operation.

Syntax: `int ErrorNo()`

Return value: The return value is the error code. For the meanings of the codes, see the listing for the `errno` function in the C runtime library reference.

FILECLOSE

The `FileClose` function closes a file handle.

Syntax: `BOOL  FileClose(iFile)`

Parameter: `iFile`

Type: `int`

Description: The file handle of the file to be closed.

Return value: The return value is TRUE if the file is open; otherwise, the return value is FALSE.

FILECOPY

Using the supplied buffer, the `FileCopy` function copies a file to another filename.

Syntax: `BOOL  FileCopy(szBuff,nSize,SrcFile,DestFile)`

Parameter: `szBuff`

Type: `LPSTR`

Description: Points to a buffer to be used when copying the file.

Parameter: `nSize`

Type: `int`

Description: The length in bytes of `szBuff`.

Parameter: `SrcFile`

Type: `LPSTR`

Description: Points to a string defining the source filename.

Parameter: `DestFile`

Type: `LPSTR`

Description: Points to a string defining the destination filename.

Return value: The return value is TRUE if the file copy is successful, FALSE if it isn't.

FILEEXISTS

The `FileExists` function determines whether a file exists.

Syntax: `BOOL  FileExists(lpFileName)`

Parameter: `lpFileName`

Type: `LPSTR`

Description: Points to a string defining the filename.

Return value: The return value is TRUE if the specified file exists, FALSE if it doesn't.

Comments: The filename can include a fully qualified drive and path specification; otherwise, the current drive and directory are used.

FILEFINDFIRST

The `FileFindFirst` function finds the first filename that matches a file specification.

Syntax:

```
HANDLE  FileFindFirst(lpszBuff, lpAttrib, szSpec,
                      iAttrib)
```

Parameter: `lpszBuff`

Type: `LPSTR`

Description: Points to a string defining the file specification.

Parameter: `lpAttrib`

Type: `LPINT`

Description: Points to an integer that will receive the file attribute of the file.

Parameter: `szSpec`

Type: `LPSTR`

Description: Points to the string to which the found filename will be written.

Parameter: `iAttrib`

Type: `int`

Description: Specifies a file attribute, which a file must match.

Return value: The return value is a local handle to a `DISKINFO` structure, which must be passed to subsequent `FileFindNext` calls. The Windows SDK `LocalLock` function can be used to obtain a pointer to this structure.

FILEFINDNEXT

The `FileFindNext` function finds subsequent files that match the file specification from the `FileFindFirst` function.

Syntax: `HANDLE  FileFindNext(szBuff,lpAttrib,hInfo)`

Parameter: `szBuff`

Type: `LPSTR`

Description: Points to a string that will receive the filename if one is found.

Parameter: `lpAttrib`

Type: `LPINT`

Description: Points to an integer to which the attribute of the file will be written.

Parameter: `hInfo`

Type: `HANDLE`

Description: The local handle to the `DISKINFO` structure returned by the `FileFindFirst` call.

Return value: The return value is a handle to the `DISKINFO` structure, which must be passed to subsequent `FileFindNext` calls.

FileGetc

The `FileGetc` function retrieves one character from an open file.

Syntax: `BOOL  FileGetc(lpValue,iFile)`

Parameter: `lpValue`

Type: `LPSTR`

Description: Points to a string to which the character will be written.

Parameter: `iFile`

Type: `int`

Description: The handle of the file.

Return value: The return value is TRUE if the character is successfully read. FALSE indicates the file isn't open or an end-of-file condition exists.

FileGetDateTime

The `FileGetDateTime` function retrieves the date and time stamp from an open file.

Syntax: `BOOL  FileGetDateTime(iHandle,lpTime,lpDate)`

Parameter: `iHandle`

Type: `int`

Description: The handle of the file.

Parameter: `lpTime`

Type: `LPINT`

Description: Points to a structure to receive the file's time stamp.

Parameter: `lpDate`

Type: `LPINT`

Description: Points to a structure to receive the file's date stamp.

Return value: The return value is TRUE if the date and time are successfully read. FALSE indicates the file isn't open.

FILEGETF

The `FileGetf` function retrieves a floating-point value from an open file.

Syntax: `BOOL  FileGetf(lpValue,iHandle)`

Parameter: `lpValue`

Type: `LPFLOAT`

Description: Points to a floating-point value to receive the data.

Parameter: `iHandle`

Type: `int`

Description: The file handle.

Return value: The return value is TRUE if the value is successfully read. FALSE indicates the file isn't open or an end-of-file condition exists.

FILEGETL

The `FileGetl` function retrieves one long integer from an open file.

Syntax: `BOOL  FileGetl(lpValue,iHandle)`

Parameter: `lpValue`

Type: `LPLONG`

Description: Points to a long integer variable to receive the data.

Parameter: `iHandle`

Type: `int`

Description: The file handle.

Return value: The return value is TRUE if the value is successfully read. FALSE indicates the file isn't open or an end-of-file condition exists.

FILEGETS

The `FileGets` function retrieves a string from an open file.

Syntax: `BOOL  FileGets(lpStr,wSize,iHandle)`

Parameter: `lpStr`

Type: `LPSTR`

Description: Points to a string to receive the data.

Parameter: `wSize`

Type: `WORD`

Description: The maximum number of characters to be placed in `lpStr`.

Parameter: `iHandle`

Type: `int`

Description: The file handle.

Return value: The return value is TRUE if the string is successfully read. FALSE indicates the file isn't open or an end-of-file condition exists.

FILEGETW

The `FileGetw` function returns a 2-byte word from an open file.

Syntax: `BOOL  FileGetw(lpValue,iHandle)`

Parameter: `lpValue`

Type: `LPINT`

Description: Points to an integer variable to receive the data.

Parameter: `iHandle`

Type: `int`

Description: The file handle.

Return value: The return value is TRUE if the value is successfully read. FALSE indicates the file isn't open or an end-of-file condition exists.

FileMultipleCopy

The `FileMultipleCopy` function copies multiple files while multitasking.

Syntax: `BOOL  FileMultipleCopy(lpSrc,lpdst)`

Parameter: `lpSrc`

Type: `LPSTR`

Description: Points to a string containing the source filespec.

Parameter: `lpdst`

Type: `LPSTR`

Description: Points to a string containing the destination filespec.

Return value: The return value is TRUE if the function is completed successfully. FALSE indicates that an error occurred.

Comments: Other Windows processes and tasks continue to run while the files are being copied, and messages are still received by the application. Care must be taken to ensure that the program issuing the `FileMultipleCopy` doesn't terminate or free the memory used by `lpSrc` or `lpdst` before the call is completed. If this happens, a UAE could result.

FILEOPEN

The `FileOpen` function opens a file.

Syntax: `BOOL  FileOpen(lpName,iOFlag,iPMode,lpHandle)`

Parameter: `lpName`

Type: `LPSTR`

Description: Points to a string containing the filename to be opened.

Parameter: `iOFlag`

Type: `int`

Description: Specifies the mode under which the file is to be opened. It can be a combination of

`O_APPEND` (append to file)
`O_BINARY` (binary file)
`O_CREAT` (create and open for write)
`O_EXCL` (do not recreate)
`O_RDONLY` (read only)
`O_RDWR` (read/write access)
`O_TEXT` (text file)
`O_TRUNC` (truncates to 0 length)
`O_WRONLY` (write only)

For more information on these flags, check the C runtime reference for the `open` command.

Parameter: `iPMode`

Type: `int`

Description: If `O_CREAT` is specified by `iOFlag`, `iPMode` specifies whether the file is to have read or write access. Valid are

```
S_IWRITE
S_IREAD
```

Parameter: `lpHandle`

Type: `LPINT`

Description: Points to an integer that receives the file handle if the open is successful.

Return value: The return value is TRUE if the file is opened successfully. FALSE indicates the file couldn't be opened.

FilePutc

The `FilePutc` function writes a single byte to an open file.

Syntax: `BOOL  FilePutc(cChar,iHandle)`

Parameter: `cChar`

Type: `char`

Description: The character to write to the file.

Parameter: `iHandle`

Type: `int`

Description: The file handle.

Return value: The return value is TRUE if the value is successfully written. FALSE indicates the file isn't open or some other error condition exists.

FilePutf

The `FilePutf` function writes a double-precision value to an open file.

Syntax: `BOOL  FilePutf(fValue,iHandle)`

Parameter: `fValue`

Type: `double`

Description: The value to write to the file.

Parameter: `iHandle`

Type: `int`

Description: The file handle.

Return value: The return value is TRUE if the value is successfully written. FALSE indicates the file isn't open or some other error condition exists.

FILEPUTL

The `FilePutl` function writes a long integer to an open file.

Syntax: `BOOL  FilePutl(lValue,iHandle)`

Parameter: `lValue`

Type: `LONG`

Description: The value to write to the file.

Parameter: `iHandle`

Type: `int`

Description: The file handle.

Return value: The return value is TRUE if the value is successfully written. FALSE indicates the file isn't open or some other error condition exists.

FILEPUTS

The `FilePuts` function writes a null-terminated string to an open file.

Syntax: `BOOL  FilePuts(lpStr,iHandle)`

Parameter: `lpStr`

Type: `LPSTR`

Description: Points to the string to be written to the file.

Parameter: `iHandle`

Type: `int`

Description: The file handle.

Return value: The return value is TRUE if the string is successfully written. FALSE indicates the file isn't open or some other error condition exists.

FILEPUTW

The `FilePutw` function writes a 2-byte word to an open file.

Syntax: `BOOL FilePutw(wValue,iHandle)`

Parameter: `wValue`

Type: `int`

Description: The value to be written to the file.

Parameter: `iHandle`

Type: `int`

Description: The file handle.

Return value: The return value is TRUE if the value is successfully written. FALSE indicates the file isn't open or some other error condition exists.

FILEREAD

The `FileRead` function reads data from an open file into a buffer.

Syntax: `WORD FileRead(lpBuff,wItemSize,wItemCount,iHandle)`

Parameter: `lpBuff`

Type: `LPVOID`

Description: Points to the buffer to receive the data.

Parameter: `wItemSize`

Type: `WORD`

Description: The size in bytes of each item.

Parameter: `wItemCount`

Type: `WORD`

Description: The number of items to write.

Parameter: `iHandle`

Type: `int`

Description: The file handle.

Return value: The return value is the number of bytes actually read. If an end-of-file condition is encountered, this might be less than the number of bytes requested.

FILEREMOVE

The `FileRemove` function removes (deletes) the specified file.

Syntax: `BOOL  FileRemove(lpFileName)`

Parameter: `lpFileName`

Type: `LPSTR`

Description: Points to a string containing the filename to be deleted.

Return value: The return value is TRUE if the filename is deleted. FALSE indicates the file isn't found or can't be deleted.

FILESEEK

The `FileSeek` function sets the read/write position of an open file.

Syntax: `BOOL  FileSeek(iHandle,lOffset,wMode)`

Parameter: `iHandle`

Type: `int`

Description: The file handle.

Parameter: `lOffset`

Type: `LONG`

Description: The desired offset.

Parameter: `wMode`

Type: `WORD`

Description: The seek mode:

> `SEEK_SET` (`lOffset` is absolute.)
> `SEEK_REL` (`lOffset` is relative to current position.)
> `SEEK_END` (`lOffset` is relative to the end of the file.)

Return value: The return value is TRUE if the seek is performed successfully. FALSE indicates the file isn't open or some other error condition exists.

FileSetDateTime

The `FileSetDateTime` function sets the date and time stamp of an open file.

Syntax: `BOOL  FileSetDateTime(iHandle,iTime,iDate)`

Parameter: `iHandle`

Type: `int`

Description: The file handle.

Parameter: `iTime`

Type: `int`

Description: The new file time (DOS format).

Parameter: `iDate`

Type: `int`

Description: The new file date (DOS format).

Return value: The return value is TRUE if the file's date and time are set successfully. FALSE indicates the file isn't found or some other error condition exists.

FILEWRITE

The `FileWrite` function writes a block of data to an open file.

Syntax: `WORD FileWrite(lpBuff,wItemSize,wItemCount,iHandle)`

Parameter: `lpBuff`

Type: `LPVOID`

Parameter: Points to a buffer containing the date.

Parameter: `wItemSize`

Type: `WORD`

Description: The size in bytes of each item.

Parameter: `wItemCount`

Type: `WORD`

Description: The number of items to write.

Parameter: `iHandle`

Type: `int`

Description: The file handle.

Return value: The return value is the number of bytes actually written. If an error condition occurs (such as disk full), this could be fewer than the bytes requested.

LISTBOX FUNCTIONS

Listbox handling under Windows is completely message-based. If you want to add or locate a string in the listbox, you must send one or more messages. The following functions perform the same tasks but eliminate the need to explicitly send the messages to the control.

TABLE 3.2. LISTBOX FUNCTIONS.

Function	*Description*
`ListAddStr`	Adds a string to the end of the listbox.
`ListDeleteStr`	Deletes a string from the listbox.
`ListFindDeleteStr`	Locates a given string in the listbox and deletes it.
`ListFindStr`	Returns the index in the listbox for a given string.
`ListGetCount`	Returns the total number of strings contained in a listbox.
`ListGetText`	Retrieves text from given character offset in the listbox.
`ListGetTextByIndex`	Retrieves text from given character offset of a listbox string.
`ListHiLiteFirstItem`	Causes top listbox string to be highlighted.
`ListReset`	Clears all data out of listbox.
`ListSelectStr`	Locates and highlights string from within listbox.

LISTADDSTR

The `ListAddStr` function adds a string to a listbox.

Syntax: `BOOL  ListAddStr(hWndList,lpStr)`

Parameter: `hWndList`

Type: `HWND`

Description: The window handle of the listbox control.

Parameter: `lpStr`

Type: `LPSTR`

Description: Points to a string to add to the listbox.

Return value: The return value is TRUE if the string can be added, FALSE if it can't.

ListDeleteStr

The `ListDeleteStr` function deletes a string from a listbox.

Syntax: `BOOL  ListDeleteStr(hWndList,iIndex)`

Parameter: `hWndList`

Type: `HWND`

Description: The window handle of the listbox control.

Parameter: `iIndex`

Type: `int`

Description: The index of the string to be deleted.

Return value: The return value is TRUE if the string is deleted. FALSE indicates the index is invalid.

Comments: Strings in a listbox are numbered beginning with zero.

ListFindDeleteStr

The `ListFindDeleteStr` function locates a string in a listbox and deletes it.

Syntax: `BOOL  ListFindDeleteStr(hWndList,lpStr)`

Parameter: `hWndList`

Type: `HWND`

Description: The window handle of the listbox control.

Parameter: `lpStr`

Type: `LPSTR`

Description: Points to the string to find and delete.

Return value: The return value is TRUE if the string is deleted. FALSE indicates the string wasn't found.

LISTFINDSTR

The `ListFindStr` function locates a string within a listbox.

Syntax: `int  ListFindStr(hWndList,lpStr,iStart)`

Parameter: `hWndList`

Type: `HWND`

Description: The window handle of the listbox control.

Parameter: `lpStr`

Type: `LPSTR`

Description: Points to the string to be located.

Parameter: `iStart`

Type: `int`

Description: The listbox index where searching is to begin.

Return value: The return value is the index of the string, or –1 (`LB_ERR`) if the index isn't found.

LISTGETCOUNT

The `ListGetCount` function returns the number of strings in a listbox.

Syntax: `int  ListGetCount(hWndList)`

Parameter: `hWndList`

Type: `HWND`

Description: The window handle of the listbox control.

Return value: The return value is the number of strings contained in the listbox.

ListGetText

The `ListGetText` function retrieves a block of text from within a listbox.

Syntax: `BOOL  ListGetText(hWndList,lpStr,iLength,iStart)`

Parameter: `hWndList`

Type: `HWND`

Description: The window handle of the listbox control.

Parameter: `lpStr`

Type: `LPSTR`

Description: Points to a string that will receive the block of text.

Parameter: `iLength`

Type: `int`

Description: The number of bytes to retrieve.

Parameter: `iStart`

Type: `int`

Description: The character index in the listbox where copying is to start.

Return value: The return value is TRUE if the entire block is transferred. FALSE indicates that the end of the listbox's data was reached before the request was satisfied.

ListGetTextByIndex

The `ListGetTextByIndex` function retrieves a block of text from within a specific string of a listbox.

Syntax: `BOOL ListGetTextByIndex(hWndList,lpStr,`
`iIndex,iLength,iStart)`

Parameter: `hWndList`

Type: `HWND`

Description: The window handle of the listbox control.

Parameter: `lpStr`

Type: `LPSTR`

Description: Points to a string that will receive the block of text.

Parameter: `iIndex`

Type: `int`

Description: Specifies the listbox line from which to retrieve the data.

Parameter: `iLength`

Type: `int`

Description: The number of characters to retrieve.

Parameter: `iStart`

Type: `int`

Description: The starting character in the specified line.

Return value: The return value is TRUE if the entire block is transferred. FALSE indicates that the end of the listbox data was reached.

ListHiLiteFirstItem

The `ListHiLiteFirstItem` function highlights (selects) the topmost item in a listbox.

Syntax: `BOOL ListHiLiteFirstItem(hWndList)`

Parameter: `hWndList`

Type: `HWND`

Description: The window handle of the listbox control.

Return value: The return value is TRUE if any strings are in the listbox.

ListReset

The `ListReset` function clears all text from a listbox.

Syntax: `BOOL ListReset(hWndList)`

Parameter: `hWndList`

Type: `HWND`

Description: The window handle of the listbox control.

Return value: The return value is always TRUE.

ListSelectStr

The `ListSelectStr` function locates a string in a listbox and highlights (selects) it.

Syntax: `BOOL ListSelectStr(hWndList,lpStr)`

Parameter: `hWndList`

Type: `HWND`

Description: The window handle of the listbox control.

Parameter: `lpStr`

Type: LPSTR

Description: Points to the string to locate and highlight.

Return value: The return value is TRUE if the string is found. FALSE indicates that it hasn't been found.

MEMORY MANIPULATION FUNCTIONS

The following functions are versions of the C runtime memory manipulation calls written to accept far and, in some cases, huge pointers.

TABLE 3.3. MEMORY MANIPULATION FUNCTIONS.

Function	*Description*
MemChr	Locates the first occurrence of a character in a memory region.
MemCmp	Compares two regions of memory.
MemCpy	Copies data between two memory regions.
MemHugecCpy	Copies data between two memory regions with terminator character.
MemHugeCmp	Compares two regions of memory (>64K).
MemHugeCpy	Copies data between two memory regions (>64K).
MemiCmp	Case-insensitive comparison of two memory regions.
MemMove	Moves data between two memory regions.
MemSet	Sets a range of memory to a given value.

MemChr

The `MemChr` function locates the first instance of a character in a memory region.

Syntax: `LPVOID  MemChr(lpMem,cChar,wSize)`

Parameter: `lpMem`

Type: `LPVOID`

Description: Points to the memory region to search.

Parameter: `cChar`

Type: `char`

Description: The character for which to search.

Parameter: `wSize`

Type: `WORD`

Description: The number of bytes to search.

Return value: The return value is a pointer to the first instance of the character, or NULL if the character isn't found.

MemCmp

The `MemCmp` function compares two memory regions.

Syntax: `int  MemCmp(lpMem1,lpMem2,wSize)`

Parameter: `lpMem1`

Type: `LPVOID`

Description: Points to the first memory region.

Parameter: `lpMem2`

Type: `LPVOID`

Description: Points to the second memory region.

Parameter: `wSize`

Type: `WORD`

Description: The number of bytes to compare.

Return value: The return value is as follows:

<0 `lpMem1` comes before `lpMem2`.
0 The regions are the same.

MemCpy

The `MemCpy` function copies data from one area of memory to another.

Syntax: `LPVOID  MemCpy(lpDest,lpSrc,wSize)`

Parameter: `lpDest`

Type: `LPVOID`

Description: Points to the destination memory region.

Parameter: `lpSrc`

Type: `LPVOID`

Description: Points to the source memory region.

Parameter: `wSize`

Type: `WORD`

Description: The number of bytes to copy.

Return value: The return value is a pointer to the destination memory region.

MemHugecCpy

The `MemHugecCpy` function copies data from one area of memory to another, specifying a terminating character.

Syntax: `HPVOID  MemHugecCpy(hpDest,hpSrc,cChar,wSize)`

Parameter: `hpDest`

Type: `HPVOID`

Description: Huge pointer to the destination memory region.

Parameter: `hpSrc`

Type: `HPVOID`

Description: Huge pointer to the source memory region.

Parameter: `cChar`

Type: `char`

Description: The terminator character.

Parameter: `wSize`

Type: `WORD`

Description: The number of bytes to copy (if the termination character isn't encountered).

Return value: The return value is a huge pointer to the destination memory region.

MEMHUGECMP

The `MemHugeCmp` function compares two memory regions (using huge pointers).

Syntax: `int  MemHugeCmp(hpMem1,hpMem2,wSize)`

Parameter: `hpMem1`

Type: `HPVOID`

Description: Pointer to the first memory region.

Parameter: `hpMem2`

Type: `HPVOID`

Description: Pointer to the second memory region.

Parameter: `wSize`

Type: `WORD`

Description: The number of bytes to compare.

Return value: The return value is as follows:

<0	`lpMem1` comes before `lpMem2`.
0	The regions are the same.
>0	`lpMem2` comes before `lpMem1`.

MemHugeCpy

The `MemHugeCpy` function copies data from one area of memory to another, using huge pointers.

Syntax: `HPVOID  MemHugeCpy(hpDest,hpSrc,wSize)`

Parameter: `hpDest`

Type: `HPVOID`

Description: Points to the destination memory region.

Parameter: `hpSrc`

Type: `HPVOID`

Description: Points to the source memory region.

Parameter: `wSize`

Type: `WORD`

Description: The number of bytes to copy.

Return value: The return value is a huge pointer to the destination string.

MemiCmp

The `MemiCmp` function performs a case-insensitive comparison of two memory regions.

Syntax: `int MemiCmp(lpMem1,lpMem2,wSize)`

Parameter: `lpMem1`

Type: `LPVOID`

Description: Points to the first memory region.

Parameter: `lpMem2`

Type: `LPVOID`

Description: Points to the second memory region.

Parameter: `wSize`

Type: `WORD`

Description: The number of bytes to compare.

Return value: The return value is as follows:

<0	`lpMem1` comes before `lpMem2`.
0	The regions are the same.
>0	`lpMem2` comes before `lpMem1`.

MemMove

The `MemMove` function moves data between two memory regions, properly handling overlap.

Syntax: `LPVOID MemMove(lpDest,lpSrc,wSize)`

Parameter: `lpDest`

Type: `LPVOID`

Description: Points to the destination memory region.

Parameter: `lpSrc`

Type: `LPVOID`

Description: Points to the source memory region.

Parameter: `wSize`

Type: `WORD`

Description: The number of bytes to move.

Return value: The return value is a pointer to the destination memory region.

Comments: This function tests the source and destination for overlap and alters the copy algorithm to ensure proper handling of the data.

MemSet

The `MemSet` function sets all bytes in a memory region to a specified byte value.

Syntax: `LPVOID  MemSet(lpDest,wChar,wSize)`

Parameter: `lpDest`

Type: `LPVOID`

Description: Points to the destination memory region.

Parameter: `wChar`

Type: `char`

Description: The character to which the data is to be set.

Parameter: `wSize`

Type: `WORD`

Description: The number of bytes to set.

Return value: The return value is a pointer to the destination memory region.

STRING FUNCTIONS

Most of the following are C runtime functions that have been rewritten to accept far data pointers, allowing them to be easily accessed by small and medium memory model programs. The remainder (marked with an asterisk) are logical extensions to these base functions.

TABLE 3.4. STRING FUNCTIONS.

Function	*Description*
`StrCat`	Concatenates (joins) two strings.
`*StrChk`	Returns pointer to start of string if non-null.
`StrChr`	Locates the occurrence of a character in a string.
`StrCmp`	Compares two strings.
`StrCpy`	Copies a string.
`*StrDeleteChar`	Deletes a character from within a string.
`*StrEnd`	Returns a pointer to the string's null terminator.
`*StrFormat`	Replaces underscores in a string with spaces.
`StriCmp`	Case-insensitive string compare.
`*StrInsertChar`	Inserts a character into a string.
`*StrIntCat`	Concatenates an integer to a string.
`*StrIntnCat`	Concatenates an integer to a fixed position in a string.
`*StrIntnCpy`	Copies an integer to a specified position of a string.

continues

TABLE 3.4. CONTINUED

Function	*Description*
`*Strip`	Removes from a string all characters in another string.
`StriStr`	Case-insensitive substring search.
`*StrLast`	Returns a pointer to the last character in a string.
`*StrLTrim`	Removes leading spaces from a string.
`StrLen`	Returns the length of a string.
`*StrLongCat`	Concatenates a long to a string.
`*StrLongnCat`	Concatenates a long to a fixed position in a string.
`*StrLongnCpy`	Copies a long to a fixed position in a string.
`StrLwr`	Converts a string to lowercase.
`StrnCat`	Concatenates a fixed number of characters.
`StrnCmp`	Compares a fixed number of characters in a string.
`StrnCpy`	Copies a fixed number of characters between strings.
`StrniCmp`	Case-insensitive compare (fixed number of characters).
`*StrnnCat`	Concatenates two strings, setting maximum length of result.
`*StrnnCpy`	Copies a string to another string.

Function	*Description*
`*StrPad`	Trims or pads a string to a set size.
`StrpBrk`	Searches a string for any occurrence of a set of characters.
`*StrpCpy`	Copies a string to another string with padding.
`*StrPrintf`	Formats a string (enhanced version of `sprintf`).
`StrrChr`	Locates last occurrence of character in string.
`*StrRemove`	Removes a section of a string.
`*StrReplace`	Replaces a section in a string with another string.
`StrRev`	Reverses a string.
`*StrRTrim`	Removes trailing spaces from a string.
`*StrScanf`	Reads values from a string (enhanced version of `sscanf`).
`StrStr`	Locates a substring in a string.
`StrTok`	Searches for tokens in a string.
`*StrTrim`	Removes leading and trailing spaces from a string.
`StrUpr`	Converts a string to uppercase.

The following functions are actually macros, which are defined in powerpak.h. All are new functions.

TABLE 3.5. STRING MACROS.

Function	*Description*
`StrEqu`	Returns TRUE if two strings are equal, FALSE if not.
`StriEqu`	Same as `StrEqu`, but case-insensitive.
`StrIntCpy`	Copies integer into a string (base 10 only).
`StrLongCpy`	Copies a long into a string (base 10 only).
`StrnEqu`	Same as `StrEqu`, but compares fixed number of characters.
`StrniEqu`	Same as `StrnEqu`, but also case-insensitive.
`StrSize`	Returns the length of the string including terminating null.

The following functions handle the conversion of numbers to strings and strings to numbers.

TABLE 3.6. STRING CONVERSION FUNCTIONS.

Function	*Description*
`FloatToEString`	Floating-point to string, scientific notation.
`FloatToFString`	Floating-point to string, decimal notation.
`IntToString`	Integer to string.
`LongToString`	Long integer to string.
`StringToFloat`	String to floating-point.
`StringToInt`	String to integer.

FLOATTOESTRING

The `FloatToEString` function converts a floating-point number to a formatted string in scientific notation.

Syntax:
```
LPSTR  FloatToEString(szBuff,dfValue,nDigit,
                      lpDecPnt,lpSign)
```

Parameter: `szBuff`

Type: `LPSTR`

Description: Points to the string that will receive the formatted number.

Parameter: `dfValue`

Type: `double`

Description: The value to be converted.

Parameter: `nDigit`

Type: `int`

Description: The total number of digits to display.

Parameter: `lpDecPnt`

Type: `LPINT`

Description: The position of the decimal point (from the left).

Parameter: `lpSign`

Type: `LPINT`

Description: A pointer to a variable, which is set to a nonzero value if `dfValue` is negative.

Return value: The return value is a pointer to the resulting string.

FLOATTOFSTRING

The `FloatToFString` function converts a floating-point number to a formatted string.

Syntax: `LPSTR FloatToFString(szBuff,dfValue,nDec,`
`lpDecPnt,lpSign)`

Parameter: `szBuff`

Type: `LPSTR`

Description: Points to the string that will receive the formatted number.

Parameter: `dfValue`

Type: `double`

Description: The value to be converted.

Parameter: `nDec`

Type: `int`

Description: The total number of digits to display.

Parameter: `lpDecPnt`

Type: `LPINT`

Description: The position of the decimal point (from the left).

Parameter: `lpSign`

Type: `LPINT`

Description: Pointer to a variable, which is set to nonzero if `dfValue` is negative.

Return value: The return value is a pointer to the resulting string.

IntToString

The `IntToString` function converts an integer to a string.

Syntax: `LPSTR  IntToString(iValue,szString)`

Parameter: `iValue`

Type: `int`

Description: The value to be converted.

Parameter: `szString`

Type: `LPSTR`

Description: Points to a string that receives the formatted number.

Return value: The return value is a pointer to the resulting string.

LongToString

The `LongToString` function converts a long integer to a string.

Syntax: `LPSTR  LongToString(lValue,lpStr)`

Parameter: `lValue`

Type: `LONG`

Description: The value to convert.

Parameter: `lpStr`

Type: `LPSTR`

Description: Points to the string in which to place the formatted number.

Return value: The return value is a pointer to the resulting string.

StrCat

The `StrCat` function concatenates two strings.

Syntax: `LPSTR  StrCat(lpszDest,lpszSrc)`

Parameter: `lpszDest`

Type: `LPSTR`

Description: Points to the destination string.

Parameter: `lpszSrc`

Type: `LPSTR`

Description: Points to the source string.

Return value: The return value is a pointer to the resulting string.

STRCHK

This function determines if a string begins with a NULL or space character.

Syntax: `LPSTR  StrChk(lpszStr)`

Parameter: `lpszStr`

Type: `LPSTR`

Description: Points to the string to be checked.

Return value: The return value is NULL if the string begins with a NULL character or space. If not, `StrChk` returns a pointer to the first character in the string.

STRCHR

The `StrChr` function locates the first occurrence of a character in a string.

Syntax: `LPSTR  StrChr(lpszStr,cChar)`

Parameter: `lpszStr`

Type: `LPSTR`

Description: Points to the string to be searched.

Parameter: `cChar`

Type: `char`

Description: The character for which to search.

Return value: The return value is a pointer to the first occurrence of the character, or NULL if the character isn't found.

StrCmp

The `StrCmp` function compares two strings.

Syntax: `int  StrCmp(lpszStr1,lpszStr2)`

Parameter: `lpszStr1`

Type: `LPSTR`

Description: Pointer to the first string.

Parameter: `lpszStr2`

Type: `LPSTR`

Description: Pointer to the second string.

Return value: The return value is one of the following:

<0	The first string occurs before the second.
0	The strings are equal.
>0	The second string occurs before the first.

StrCpy

The `StrCpy` function copies one string to another.

Syntax: `LPSTR  StrCpy(lpszDest,lpszSrc)`

Parameter: `lpszDest`

Type: `LPSTR`

Description: Points to the destination string.

Parameter: `lpszSrc`

Type: `LPSTR`

Description: Points to the source string.

Return value: The return value is a pointer to the destination string.

StrDeleteChar

The `StrDeleteChar` function deletes the character at the given offset in the string.

Syntax: `LPSTR StrDeleteChar(lpszStr,iStart)`

Parameter: `lpszStr`

Type: `LPSTR`

Description: Points to the string to be processed.

Parameter: `iStart`

Type: `int`

Description: The offset in `lpszStr` of the character to be deleted.

Return value: The return value is a pointer to the destination string.

StrEnd

The `StrEnd` function returns a pointer to the null terminator at the end of a string.

Syntax: `LPSTR StrEnd(lpszStr)`

Parameter: `lpszStr`

Type: `LPSTR`

Description: Points to the string to be processed.

Return value: The return value is a pointer to the string's null terminator.

StrEqu

This function compares two strings and returns TRUE if they are equal.

Syntax: `BOOL StrEqu(lpszStr1,lpszStr2)`

Parameter: `lpszStr1`

Type: `LPSTR`

Description: Points to the first string.

Parameter: `lpszStr2`

Type: `LPSTR`

Description: Points to the second string.

Return value: The return value is TRUE if the strings are equal, FALSE if they aren't.

Comments: This function is actually defined as a macro in powerpak.h.

StrFormat

The `StrFormat` function removes all spaces from a string and replaces all underscores with spaces.

Syntax: `LPSTR  StrFormat(lpszStr)`

Parameter: `lpszStr`

Type: `LPSTR`

Description: Points to the string to be processed.

Return value: The return value is a pointer to the beginning of the string.

StriCmp

The `StriCmp` function compares two strings, disregarding case.

Syntax: `int  StriCmp(lpszStr1,lpszStr2)`

Parameter: `lpszStr1`

Type: `LPSTR`

Description: Points to the first string.

Parameter: `lpszStr2`

Type: `LPSTR`

Description: Points to the second string.

Return value: The return value is one of the following:

<0	The first string occurs before the second.
0	The strings are equivalent.
>0	The second string occurs before the first.

STRIEQU

The `StriEqu` function compares two strings (disregarding case) and returns TRUE if they are equal.

Syntax: `BOOL  StriEqu(lpszStr1,lpszStr2)`

Parameter: `lpszStr1`

Type: `LPSTR`

Description: Points to the first string.

Parameter: `lpszStr2`

Type: `LPSTR`

Description: Points to the second string.

Return value: The return value is TRUE if the strings are equal, FALSE if they aren't.

Comments: This function is actually defined as a macro in powerpak.h.

STRINGTOFLOAT

The `StringToFloat` function converts a string to a floating-point number.

Syntax: `double  StringToFloat(lpszStr)`

Parameter: `lpszStr`

Type: `LPSTR`

Description: Points to the string to be converted.

Return value: The return value is the floating-point representation of the string. If the string doesn't represent a valid floating-point number, the return value is zero.

Comments: If the string doesn't contain a valid number, the function returns zero.

StringToInt

The `StringToInt` function converts a string to an integer number.

Syntax: `int StringToInt(lpszStr)`

Parameter: `lpszStr`

Type: `LPSTR`

Description: Points to the string to be converted.

Return value: The return value is the integer representation of the string. If the string doesn't represent a valid integer number, the return value is zero.

Comments: If the string doesn't contain a valid number, the function returns zero.

StringToLong

The `StringToLong` function converts a string to a long integer.

Syntax: `long StringToLong(lpszStr)`

Parameter: `lpszStr`

Type: `LPSTR`

Description: Points to the string to be converted.

Return value: The return value is the long integer representation of the string. If the string doesn't represent a valid long integer number, the return value is zero.

Comments: If the string doesn't contain a valid number, the function returns zero.

StrInsertChar

The `StrInsertChar` function inserts a character at a given position in a string.

Syntax: `LPSTR  StrInsertChar(cChar,lpszString,iInsertPos)`

Parameter: `cChar`

Type: `char`

Description: The character to insert.

Parameter: `lpszString`

Type: `LPSTR`

Description: Points to the string to be processed.

Parameter: `iInsertPos`

Type: `int`

Description: The position in `lpszString` where the insertion is to be made.

Return value: The return value is a pointer to the beginning of the string.

StrIntCat

This function converts an integer to a string and appends it to the end of another string.

Syntax: `LPSTR  StrIntCat(lpStr,iInt)`

Parameter: `lpStr`

Type: `LPSTR`

Description: Points to the destination string.

Parameter: `iInt`

Type: `int`

Description: The value to be appended.

Return value: The return value is a pointer to the beginning of the string.

StrIntCpy

The `StrIntCpy` function converts an integer to a string and copies it to another string.

Syntax: `LPSTR  StrIntCpy(lpszStr,iInt)`

Parameter: `lpszStr`

Type: `LPSTR`

Description: Points to the destination string.

Parameter: `iInt`

Type: `int`

Description: The value to be converted and copied.

Return value: The return value is a pointer to the beginning of the string.

StrIntnCat

The `StrIntnCat` function converts an integer to a string and appends it to the end of another string. A maximum length for the resulting string is specified.

Syntax: `LPSTR  StrIntnCat(lpszStr,iInt,iMaxChars)`

Parameter: `lpszStr`

Type: `LPSTR`

Description: Points to the destination string.

Parameter: `iInt`

Type: `int`

Description: The value to be appended.

Parameter: `iMaxChars`

Type: `int`

Description: The maximum length of the string.

Return value: The return value is a pointer to the beginning of the string.

StrIntnCpy

The `StrIntnCpy` function converts an integer to a string and copies it to another string. A maximum length for the resulting string is specified.

Syntax: `LPSTR StrIntnCpy(lpszStr,iInt,iMaxChars)`

Parameter: `lpszStr`

Type: `LPSTR`

Description: Points to the destination string.

Parameter: `iInt`

Type: `int`

Description: The value to be appended.

Parameter: `iMaxChars`

Type: `int`

Description: The maximum length of the string.

Return value: The return value is a pointer to the beginning of the string.

STRIP

The `Strip` function removes from a string all occurrences of characters found in a second string.

Syntax: `LPSTR  Strip(lpszStr1,lpszStr2)`

Parameter: `lpszStr1`

Type: `LPSTR`

Description: Points to the string to be processed.

Parameter: `lpszStr2`

Type: `LPSTR`

Description: Points to the string containing the characters to be stripped.

Return value: The return value is a pointer to the beginning of the string.

STRISTR

The `StriStr` function locates the first occurrence of a substring in another string, ignoring case differences.

Syntax: `LPSTR  StriStr(lpszStr1,lpszStr2)`

Parameter: `lpszStr1`

Type: `LPSTR`

Description: Points to the main string.

Parameter: `lpszStr2`

Type: `LPSTR`

Description: Points to the substring.

Return value: The return value is a pointer to the beginning of the second string in the first string, or NULL if the substring isn't found.

StrLast

The `StrLast` function returns a pointer to the last character of a string.

Syntax: `LPSTR  StrLast(lpszStr)`

Parameter: `lpszStr`

Type: `LPSTR`

Description: Points to the string to be processed.

Return value: The return value is a pointer to the last character in the string. If the string is empty, the return value is the pointer to the null character.

StrLen

The `StrLen` function returns the length of a string.

Syntax: `int  StrLen(lpszStr)`

Parameter: `lpszStr`

Type: `LPSTR`

Description: Points to the string to be processed.

Return value: The return value is the length (in characters) of the string.

StrLongCat

The `StrLongCat` function converts a long integer to a string and appends it to the end of another string.

Syntax: `LPSTR  StrLongCat(lpszStr,lLong)`

Parameter: `lpszStr`

Type: `LPSTR`

Description: Points to the destination string.

Parameter: `lLong`

Type: `LONG`

Description: The value to be appended.

Return value: The return value is a pointer to the resulting string.

STRLONGCPY

The `StrLongCpy` function converts a long integer to a string and copies the result to another string.

Syntax: `LPSTR  StrLongCpy(lpszStr,lLong)`

Parameter: `lpszStr`

Type: `LPSTR`

Description: Points to the destination string.

Parameter: `lLong`

Type: `LONG`

Description: The value to be converted and copied.

Return value: The return value is a pointer to the resulting string.

STRLONGNCAT

The `StrLongnCat` function converts a long integer to a string and appends it to the end of another string. A maximum length for the resulting string is specified.

Syntax: `LPSTR  StrLongnCat(lpszStr,lLong,iMaxChars)`

Parameter: `lpszStr`

Type: `LPSTR`

Description: Points to the destination string.

Parameter: `lLong`

Type: `LONG`

Description: The value to be appended.

Parameter: `iMaxChars`

Type: `int`

Description: The maximum length of the string.

Return value: The return value is a pointer to the resulting string.

STRLONGNCPY

The `StrLongnCpy` function converts a long integer to a string and copies the result to another string. A maximum length for the resulting string is specified.

Syntax: `LPSTR  StrLongnCpy(lpszStr,lLong,iMaxChars)`

Parameter: `lpszStr`

Type: `LPSTR`

Description: Points to the destination string.

Parameter: `lLong`

Type: `LONG`

Description: The value to be converted and copied.

Parameter: `iMaxChars`

Type: `int`

Description: The maximum length of the string.

Return value: The return value is a pointer to the resulting string.

STRLTRIM

The `StrLTrim` function removes all leading spaces from a string.

Syntax: `LPSTR  StrLTrim(lpszStr)`

Parameter: `lpszStr`

Type: `LPSTR`

Description: Points to the string to be processed.

Return value: The return value is a pointer to the beginning of the string.

StrLwr

The `StrLwr` function converts all uppercase letters in a string to lowercase.

Syntax: `LPSTR  StrLwr(lpszStr)`

Parameter: `lpszStr`

Type: `LPSTR`

Description: Points to the string to be processed.

Return value: The return value is a pointer to the beginning of the string.

StrnCat

The `StrnCat` function appends one string to another, specifying a maximum length for the resulting string.

Syntax: `LPSTR  StrnCat(lpszDest,lpszSrc,iMaxChars)`

Parameter: `lpszDest`

Type: `LPSTR`

Description: Points to the destination string.

Parameter: `lpszSrc`

Type: `LPSTR`

Description: Points to the source string.

Parameter: `iMaxChars`

Type: `int`

Description: The maximum length of the destination string.

Return value: The return value is a pointer to the beginning of the destination string.

StrnCmp

The `StrnCmp` function compares two strings, considering only a specified number of characters.

Syntax: `int  StrnCmp(lpszStr1,lpszStr2,iMaxChars)`

Parameter: `lpszStr1`

Type: `LPSTR`

Description: Points to the first string.

Parameter: `lpszStr2`

Type: `LPSTR`

Description: Points to the second string.

Parameter: `iMaxChars`

Type: `int`

Description: The number of characters to compare.

Return value: The return value is one of the following:

<0	The first string occurs before the second.
0	The strings are equal.
>0	The second string occurs before the first.

StrnCpy

The `StrnCpy` function copies a specified number of bytes from one string to another string.

Syntax: `LPSTR  StrnCpy(lpszDest,lpszSrc,iMaxChars)`

Parameter: `lpszDest`

Type: `LPSTR`

Description: Points to the destination string.

Parameter: `lpszSrc`

Type: `LPSTR`

Description: Points to the source string.

Parameter: `iMaxChars`

Type: `int`

Description: The maximum length of the destination string.

Return value: The return value is a pointer to the destination string.

STRNEQU

The `StrnEqu` function compares a specified number of bytes from two strings, returning TRUE if they are equal.

Syntax: `BOOL  StrnEqu(lpszStr1,lpszStr2,iMaxChars)`

Parameter: `lpszStr1`

Type: `LPSTR`

Description: Points to the first string.

Parameter: `lpszStr2`

Type: `LPSTR`

Description: Points to the second string.

Parameter: `iMaxChars`

Type: `int`

Description: The number of characters to compare.

Return value: The return value is TRUE if the substrings are equal, FALSE if they aren't.

Comments: This function is actually defined as a macro in powerpak.h.

STRNICMP

This function compares a specified number of bytes from two strings, ignoring case differences.

Syntax: `int  StrniCmp(lpszStr1,lpszStr2,iMaxChars)`

Parameter: `lpszStr1`

Type: `LPSTR`

Description: Points to the first string.

Parameter: `lpszStr2`

Type: `LPSTR`

Description: Points to the second string.

Parameter: `iMaxChars`

Type: `int`

Description: The number of characters to compare.

Return value: The return value is one of the following:

<0	The first string occurs before the second.
0	The strings are equivalent.
>0	The second string occurs before the first.

STRNIEQU

The `StrniEqu` function compares a specified number of bytes of two strings, ignoring case differences, and returns TRUE if they are equal.

Syntax: `BOOL  StrniEqu(lpszStr1,lpszStr2,iMaxChars)`

Parameter: `lpszStr1`

Type: `LPSTR`

Description: Points to the first string.

Parameter: `lpszStr2`

Type: `LPSTR`

Description: Points to the second string.

Parameter: `iMaxChars`

Type: `int`

Description: The number of characters to compare.

Return value: The return value is TRUE if the strings are equal, FALSE if they aren't.

Comments: This function is actually defined as a macro in powerpak.h.

STRNNCAT

The `StrnnCat` function appends characters from one string to another until the resulting string reaches a specified length.

Syntax: `LPSTR  StrnnCat(lpszDest,lpszSrc,iMaxChars)`

Parameter: `lpszDest`

Type: `LPSTR`

Description: Points to the destination string.

Parameter: `lpszSrc`

Type: `LPSTR`

Description: Points to the source string.

Parameter: `iMaxChars`

Type: `int`

Description: The target length of the specified string.

Return value: The return value is a pointer to the destination string.

STRNNCPY

The `StrnnCpy` function copies text from one string to another until the destination string reaches a specified length.

Syntax: `LPSTR  StrnnCpy(lpszDest,lpszSrc,iMaxChars)`

Parameter: `lpszDest`

Type: `LPSTR`

Description: Points to the destination string.

Parameter: `lpszSrc`

Type: `LPSTR`

Description: Points to the source string.

Parameter: `iMaxChars`

Type: `int`

Description: The target length of the destination string.

Return value: The return value is a pointer to the destination string.

STRPAD

The `StrPad` function trims or pads a string to a specified length.

Syntax: `LPSTR  StrPad(lpszStr,iNumChars)`

Parameter: `lpszStr`

Type: `LPSTR`

Description: Points to the string to be processed.

Parameter: `iNumChars`

Type: `int`

Description: The target length of the string.

Return value: The return value is a pointer to the beginning of the string.

StrpBrk

The `StrpBrk` function locates the first occurrence of any of the characters in another string.

Syntax: `LPSTR  StrpBrk(lpszStr1,lpszStr2)`

Parameter: `lpszStr1`

Type: `LPSTR`

Description: Points to the string to be processed.

Parameter: `lpszStr2`

Type: `LPSTR`

Description: Points to the string containing the characters for which to search.

Return value: The return value is a pointer to the first occurrence of any of the characters, or NULL if none of the characters are found.

StrpCpy

The `StrpCpy` function copies text from one string to another, padding the resulting string to a specified length.

Syntax: `LPSTR  StrpCpy(lpszDest,lpszSrc,iChars)`

Parameter: `lpszDest`

Type: `LPSTR`

Description: Points to the destination string.

Parameter: `lpszSrc`

Type: `LPSTR`

Description: Points to the source string.

Parameter: `iChars`

Type: `int`

Description: The target length of the destination string.

Return value: The return value is a pointer to the destination string.

STRPRINTF

The `StrPrintf` function is a far pointer version of the C runtime `sprintf` function. For comprehensive information on using `StrPrintf`, consult the C runtime library manual.

Syntax: `int  StrPrintf(lpBuffer,lpFormat,[Args])`

Parameter: `lpBuffer`

Type: `LPSTR`

Description: Points to the buffer to receive the formatted string.

Parameter: `lpFormat`

Type: `LPSTR`

Description: Points to the string defining the text to be printed.

Parameter: `[Args]`

Type: See the C runtime library.

Description: A variable number of arguments to be inserted into `lpFormat`.

Return value: The return value is the number of characters that are placed in `lpBuffer`.

STRRCHR

This function locates the last occurrence of a character in a string.

Syntax: `LPSTR  StrrChr(lpszStr,cChar)`

Parameter: `lpszStr`

Type: `LPSTR`

Description: Points to the string to be processed.

Parameter: `cChar`

Type: `char`

Description: The character for which to search.

Return value: The return value is a pointer to the last occurrence of the character, or NULL if the character isn't found.

STRREMOVE

The `StrRemove` function removes a section of a string.

Syntax: `LPSTR  StrRemove(lpszStr,iFrom,iTo)`

Parameter: `lpszStr`

Type: `LPSTR`

Description: Points to the string to be processed.

Parameter: `iFrom`

Type: `int`

Description: The starting offset in the string.

Parameter: `iTo`

Type: `int`

Description: The ending offset in the string.

Return value: The return value is a pointer to the beginning of the string.

StrReplace

The `StrReplace` function substitutes characters in a string using the guide in another string.

Syntax: `LPSTR  StrReplace(lpszOld,lpszNew)`

Parameter: `lpszOld`

Type: `LPSTR`

Description: Points to the string to be processed.

Parameter: `lpszNew`

Type: `LPSTR`

Description: Points to a string containing the characters to be replaced and their replacements.

Return value: The return value is a pointer to the beginning of the string.

Comments: The `lpszNew` string contains couples of characters. The first character is the one to be replaced, and the second character is the replacement.

StrRev

The `StrRev` function reverses the order of the characters in a string.

Syntax: `LPSTR  StrRev(lpszStr)`

Parameter: `lpszStr`

Type: `LPSTR`

Description: Points to the string to be processed.

Return value: The return value is a pointer to the beginning of the string.

StrRTrim

The `StrRTrim` function removes all trailing spaces from a string.

Syntax: `LPSTR  StrRTrim(lpszStr)`

Parameter: `lpszStr`

Type: `LPSTR`

Description: Points to the string to be processed.

Return value: The return value is a pointer to the beginning of the string.

StrScanf

The `StrScanf` function is a far pointer version of the C runtime function `sscanf`.

Syntax: `int  StrScanf(lpStr,lpFormat,[Args])`

Parameter: `lpStr`

Type: `LPSTR`

Description: Points to the string to be processed.

Parameter: `lpFormat`

Type: `LPSTR`

Description: Points to the string containing the formatting codes.

Parameter: `[Args]`

Type: See the C runtime library.

Description: A variable number of arguments to receive the data collected from `lpStr`.

Return value: The return value specifies the number of fields converted.

STRSIZE

The `StrSize` function returns the true size of a string, including the terminating null.

Syntax: `int  StrSize(lpszStr)`

Parameter: `lpszStr`

Type: `LPSTR`

Description: Points to the string to be processed.

Return value: The return value is the size of the string, including the terminating null.

STRSTR

The `StrStr` function locates the first occurrence of a substring in a string.

Syntax: `LPSTR  StrStr(lpszStr1,lpszStr2)`

Parameter: `lpszStr1`

Type: `LPSTR`

Description: Points to the main string.

Parameter: `lpszStr2`

Type: `LPSTR`

Description: Points to the substring.

Return value: The return value is a pointer to the first occurrence of the second string within the first, or NULL if not found.

STRTOK

The `StrTok` function breaks a delimited string into substrings.

Syntax: `LPSTR  StrTok(lpszStr,lpszTokens)`

Parameter: `lpszStr`

Type: `LPSTR`

Description: Points to the string to be broken.

Parameter: `lpszTokens`

Type: `LPSTR`

Description: Points to a string containing the valid tokens.

Return value: The return value is a pointer to the first or subsequent subfields in the string.

Comments: For more information on the uses of `StrTok`, consult the C reference manual.

STRTRIM

The `StrTrim` function removes leading and trailing spaces from a string.

Syntax: `LPSTR StrTrim(lpszStr)`

Parameter: `lpszStr`

Type: `LPSTR`

Description: Points to the string to be processed.

Return value: The return value is a pointer to the beginning of the string.

STRUPR

The `StrUpr` function converts all lowercase letters in a string to uppercase.

Syntax: `LPSTR StrUpr(lpszStr)`

Parameter: `lpszStr`

Type: LPSTR

Description: Points to the string to be processed.

Return value: The return value is a pointer to the beginning of the string.

SYSTEM FUNCTIONS

The following functions provide access to system and file-related functions not supported by SDK functions. Most of them provide the functionality of MS-DOS Int 21 calls without having to resort to assembly language. These functions all require data to be passed in far pointers.

TABLE 3.7. SYSTEM FUNCTIONS.

Function	*Description*
FullMkDir	Creates a full directory path.
GetCPUType	Returns the type of the CPU.
GetFileString	Searches a file for a specific profile string.
SysCreateSubDir	Creates a subdirectory.
SysDeleteFile	Deletes a file.
SysDeleteSubDir	Removes a subdirectory.
SysDiskBytesFree	Returns bytes free on disk.
SysDiskBytesTotal	Returns total bytes on disk.
SysDiskInfo	Returns table of disk information.
SysExecPgm	Executes another Windows program.
SysFileSpec	Determines if filename matches a wildcard filespec.

Function	*Description*
`SysFindFirst`	Finds first file in a directory that matches filespec.
`SysFindNext`	Finds next file in a directory that matches filespec.
`SysFixedDrive`	Determines if specified drive is a fixed (local) drive.
`SysGetCurrentDir`	Copies the current directory into a string.
`SysGetDTA`	Retrieves the current disk transfer address.
`SysGetDate`	Retrieves current date in standard DOS format.
`SysGetDefDrive`	Returns the current default drive.
`SysGetFileAttr`	Retrieves the attributes of the specified file.
`SysGetLogicalDriveCount`	Returns the number of drives accessible to the system.
`SysGetTime`	Retrieves current time in standard DOS format.
`SysGetVolumeName`	Retrieves the volume name of a disk.
`SysMakePath`	Assembles a path string.
`SysNetworkDrive`	Determines if specified drive is a network (remote) drive.
`SysRead`	Reads specified number of bytes from a file handle.
`SysRenameFile`	Renames a file.
`SysSetCurrentDir`	Makes specified path the current directory.
`SysSetDTA`	Sets the disk transfer address.
`SysSetDate`	Sets the current date.

continues

TABLE 3.7. CONTINUED

Function	*Description*
`SysSetDefDrive`	Sets the current default drive.
`SysSetFileAttr`	Changes the attributes of the specified file.
`SysSetTime`	Sets the current time.
`SysSetVolumeName`	Sets the current volume name of the disk.
`SysSplitPath`	Splits a drive/path/file string into its components.
`SysValidDrive`	Determines if specified drive is legal.
`SysWrite`	Writes a specified number of bytes to a file handle.
`SysXCreateFile`	Creates a file and returns a file handle.
`WriteFileString`	Writes a profile string to a file.

FullMkDir

The `FullMkDir` function creates the specified path, including all parent directories.

Syntax: `BOOL  FullMkDir(lpPath)`

Parameter: `lpPath`

Type: `LPSTR`

Description: A pointer to a string containing the path.

Return value: The return value is TRUE if the directory path is successfully created.

GETCPUTYPE

The `GetCPUType` function retrieves the CPU type of the host machine.

Syntax: `CPUID  GetCPUType()`

Return value: The return value specifies the CPU type:

0 8086 or 8088
1 80186 or 80188
2 80286
3 80386 or 80486

GETFILESTRING

The `GetFileString` function retrieves a profile string from a user file.

Syntax:
```
int  GetFileString(lpszKey,lpszDefault,
     lpReturn,nSize,lpszFile)
```

Parameter: `lpszKey`

Type: `LPSTR`

Description: Points to the key name for the value to be retrieved.

Parameter: `lpszDefault`

Type: `LPSTR`

Description: Points to a string defining the default value to be used if the key value can't be found.

Parameter: `lpReturn`

Type: `LPSTR`

Description: Points to a string that receives the value of the key.

Parameter: `nSize`

Type: `int`

Description: The maximum number of characters to be placed in `lpReturn`.

Parameter: `lpszFile`

Type: `LPSTR`

Description: A pointer to a string containing the filename to be searched.

Return value: The return value is the number of characters copied into the return string, or 0 if the key isn't found.

Comments: This function scans the specified file for the first line beginning with the key string (with an equal sign appended to it). It then copies whatever is to the right of the equal sign to `lpReturn`. If no matching string is found, the string specified by `pzDefault` is copied.

SysCreateSubDir

The `SysCreateSubDir` function creates the specified subdirectory.

Syntax: `int SysCreateSubDir(lpszNewSubDir)`

Parameter: `lpszNewSubDir`

Type: `LPSTR`

Description: Points to a string containing the path to create.

Return value: The return value is an error code. Zero indicates that the directory was successfully created. Possible error codes:

3	path not found
5	access denied
6, 16	specified path is the current directory

SysDeleteFile

The `SysDeleteFile` function deletes the specified file.

Syntax: `int SysDeleteFile(lpszExistingFile)`

Parameter: `lpszExistingFile`

Type: `LPSTR`

Description: Points to a string containing the file to delete.

Return value: The return value is an error code. 0 indicates that the file was successfully deleted. Any other value indicates that the file couldn't be deleted.

SysDeleteSubDir

The `SysDeleteSubDir` function deletes an existing subdirectory.

Syntax: `int  SysDeleteSubDir(lpszExistingDir)`

Parameter: `lpszExistingDir`

Type: `LPSTR`

Description: Points to a string containing the subdirectory to be deleted.

Return value: The return value is an error code. 0 indicates that the subdirectory was successfully deleted. Possible error codes:

3	path not found
5	access denied
6, 16	specified path is the current directory

Comments: A subdirectory can't be deleted unless it is empty and has no child subdirectories.

SysDiskBytesFree

The `SysDiskBytesFree` function returns the number of bytes free on a floppy or hard disk.

Syntax: `DWORD  SysDiskBytesFree(iDrive)`

Parameter: `iDrive`

Type: `int`

Description: The drive to check (0=current, 1=A, 2=B, and so forth).

Return value: The return value is the number of bytes free on the disk.

SysDiskBytesTotal

The `SysDiskBytesTotal` function returns the total capacity of a floppy or hard disk in bytes.

Syntax: `DWORD  SysDiskBytesTotal(iDrive)`

Parameter: `iDrive`

Type: `int`

Description: The drive to check (0=current, 1=A, 2=B, and so forth).

Return value: The return value is the total capacity of the disk.

SysDiskInfo

The `SysDiskInfo` function returns specific information about a drive.

Syntax: `VOID  SysDiskInfo(iDrive,lpDiskInfo)`

Parameter: `iDrive`

Type: `int`

Description: The drive to check (0=current, 1=A, 2=B, and so forth).

Parameter: `lpDiskInfo`

Type: `LPDISKINFO`

Description: Points to a structure that contains the disk information.

SysFileSpec

The `SysFileSpec` function determines whether a filename matches a given wildcard filespec.

Syntax: `BOOL  SysFileSpec(lpszPattern,lpszFileName)`

Parameter: `lpszPattern`

Type: `LPSTR`

Description: Points to a string containing the filespec.

Parameter: `lpszFileName`

Type: `LPSTR`

Description: Points to a string containing the filename to be tested.

Return value: The return value is TRUE if the filename matches the filespec, FALSE if it doesn't.

SysFindFirst

The `SysFindFirst` function finds the first occurrence of a wildcard filespec in a directory.

Syntax: `int  SysFindFirst(iAttrib,lpszPath,lpFileInfo)`

Parameter: `iAttrib`

Type: `int`

Description: The required attribute for a file to match.

Parameter: `lpszPath`

Type: `LPSTR`

Description: Points to a string containing the wildcard specification.

Parameter: `lpFileInfo`

Type: `LPFILEINFO`

Description: Points to a structure that contains the specifics about the found file.

Return value: The return value is zero if a file is found, nonzero if not.

SYSFINDNEXT

The `SysFindNext` function finds subsequent files that match the filespec specified in the `SysFindFirst` call.

Syntax: `int   SysFindNext(lpFileInfo)`

Parameter: `lpFileInfo`

Type: `LPFILEINFO`

Description: Points to the structure returned by the `SysFindFirst` call.

Return value: The return value is zero if another matching file is found; if not, the return value is 18.

SYSFIXEDDRIVE

The `SysFixedDrive` function returns TRUE if the drive in question is a fixed (local) drive.

Syntax: `BOOL   SysFixedDrive(iDrive)`

Parameter: `iDrive`

Type: `int`

Description: The drive to check (0=current, 1=A, 2=B, and so forth).

Return value: The return value is TRUE if the specified drive is a local fixed drive, FALSE if not.

SysGetCurrentDir

The `SysGetCurrentDir` function returns the currently active directory.

Syntax: `BOOL  SysGetCurrentDir(iDrive,lpszCurrentDir)`

Parameter: `iDrive`

Type: `int`

Description: The drive to check (0=current, 1=A, 2=B, and so forth).

Parameter: `lpszCurrentDir`

Type: `LPSTR`

Description: Points to a string that contains the current directory name.

Return value: The return value is TRUE if the function is successful, FALSE if not.

SysGetDate

The `SysGetDate` function retrieves the DOS date.

Syntax: `VOID  SysGetDate(lpDay,lpMonth,lpYear)`

Parameter: `lpDay`

Type: `LPINT`

Description: Points to a variable to receive the day.

Parameter: `lpMonth`

Type: `LPINT`

Description: Points to a variable to receive the month.

Parameter: `lpYear`

Type: `LPINT`

Description: Points to a variable to receive the year.

SysGetDefDrive

The `SysGetDefDrive` function returns the currently active drive.

Syntax: `int SysGetDefDrive()`

Return value: The return value is the ID of the default drive (0=A, 1=B, 2=C, and so forth).

SysGetDTA

The `SysGetDTA` function returns a pointer to the current disk transfer address.

Syntax: `LPVOID SysGetDTA()`

Return value: The return value is a pointer to the current disk transfer address.

SysGetFileAttr

The `SysGetFileAttr` function retrieves the DOS file attributes for a given file.

Syntax: `int SysGetFileAttr(lpszPath,lpAttrib)`

Parameter: `lpszPath`

Type: `LPSTR`

Description: Points to a string containing the fully qualified filename.

Parameter: `lpAttrib`

Type: `LPWORD`

Description: Points to a variable that contains the attribute word for the file (if found).

Return value: The return value is the attribute word for the specified file. A zero return indicates that the file isn't found.

SysGetLogicalDriveCount

The `SysGetLogicalDriveCount` function returns the number of logical drives known to DOS.

Syntax: `int SysGetLogicalDriveCount()`

Return value: The return value is the number of logical drives.

SysGetTime

The `SysGetTime` function retrieves the DOS time.

Syntax: `VOID SysGetTime(lpHour,lpMinute,lpSecond)`

Parameter: `lpHour`

Type: `LPINT`

Description: Points to a variable to receive the hour.

Parameter: `lpMinute`

Type: `LPINT`

Description: Points to a variable to receive the minute.

Parameter: `lpSecond`

Type: `LPINT`

Description: Points to a variable to receive the second.

SysGetVolumeName

The `SysGetVolumeName` function retrieves the volume name of the specified drive.

Syntax: `BOOL SysGetVolumeName(iDrive,lpszVolumeName)`

Parameter: `iDrive`

Type: `int`

Description: The drive to check (0=current, 1=A, 2=B, and so forth).

Parameter: `lpszVolumeName`

Type: `LPSTR`

Description: Points to the string that will contain the volume name, if found.

Return value: The return value is TRUE if there is a volume name entry for the drive in question, FALSE if not.

SysMakePath

The `SysMakePath` function creates the specified path from its component parts.

Syntax:

```
LPSTR  SysMakePath(lpszPath,lpszDrive,lpszDir,
       lpszName,lpszExt)
```

Parameter: `lpszPath`

Type: `LPSTR`

Description: Points to a string that will contain the completed filename.

Parameter: `lpszDrive`

Type: `LPSTR`

Description: Points to a string containing the drive.

Parameter: `lpszDir`

Type: `LPSTR`

Description: Points to a string containing the directory path.

Parameter: `lpszName`

Type: `LPSTR`

Description: Points to a string containing the filename.

Parameter: `lpszExt`

Type: `LPSTR`

Description: Points to a string containing the extension.

Return value: The return value is a pointer to the path string.

SysNetworkDrive

The `SysNetworkDrive` function returns TRUE if the drive in question is a network (remote) drive.

Syntax: `BOOL  SysNetworkDrive(iDrive)`

Parameter: `iDrive`

Type: `int`

Description: The drive to check (0=current, 1=A, 2=B, and so forth).

Return value: The return value is TRUE if the drive is a network drive.

SysRead

The `SysRead` function reads a block of data from an open file.

Syntax: `int  SysRead(iHandle,lpBuff,uSize,lpRead)`

Parameter: `iHandle`

Type: `int`

Description: The handle to the file.

Parameter: `lpBuff`

Type: `LPVOID`

Description: The pointer to the buffer to receive the data.

Parameter: `uSize`

Type: `WORD`

Description: The number of bytes to read.

Parameter: `lpRead`

Type: `LPWORD`

Description: Points to a variable that will receive the number of bytes actually read.

Return value: The return value is the number of bytes actually read by the operation.

SysRenameFile

The `SysRenameFile` function renames a file.

Syntax: `int   SysRenameFile(lpszOldFile,lpszNewFile)`

Parameter: `lpszOldFile`

Type: `LPSTR`

Description: Points to a string containing the existing filename.

Parameter: `lpszNewFile`

Type: `LPSTR`

Description: Points to a string containing the new filename.

Return value: The return value is zero if the file is successfully renamed, nonzero if an error occurs (file not found, file already exists, and so on).

SysSetCurrentDir

The `SysSetCurrentDir` function makes a specified path the current directory for disk operations.

Syntax: `int   SysSetCurrentDir(lpszNewDir)`

Parameter: `lpszNewDir`

Type: `LPSTR`

Description: Points to a string containing the directory path.

Return value: The return value is zero if the function is completed successfully; nonzero indicates the path doesn't exist or couldn't be located.

SysSetDate

The `SysSetDate` function sets the system date.

Syntax: `BOOL  SysSetDate(iDay,iMonth,iYear)`

Parameter: `iDay`

Type: `int`

Description: The day.

Parameter: `iMonth`

Type: `int`

Description: The month.

Parameter: `iYear`

Type: `int`

Description: The year.

SysSetDefDrive

The `SysSetDefDrive` function makes the specified drive the default for disk operations.

Syntax: `int  SysSetDefDrive(iDrive)`

Parameter: `iDrive`

Type: `int`

Description: The drive to set (0=A, 1=B, and so forth).

Return value: The return value is zero if the function is successful; if not, it is a nonzero value.

SysSetDTA

The `SysSetDTA` function sets the Disk Transfer Address.

Syntax: `VOID  SysSetDTA(lpDTA)`

Parameter: `lpDTA`

Type: `LPVOID`

Description: Pointer to the new Disk Transfer Address.

SysSetFileAttr

The `SysSetFileAttr` function sets a file's attributes.

Syntax: `int  SysSetFileAttr(lpszPath,wAttrib)`

Parameter: `lpszPath`

Type: `LPSTR`

Description: Points to a string containing the filename.

Parameter: `wAttrib`

Type: `WORD`

Description: The new attributes for the file.

Return value: The return value is zero if the function is successful; if not, it is a nonzero value. The most likely reason for failure is that the file couldn't be found.

SysSetTime

The `SysSetTime` function sets the system time.

Syntax: `BOOL  SysSetTime(iHour,iMinute,iSeconds)`

Parameter: `iHour`

Type: `int`

Description: The hour.

Parameter: `iMinute`

Type: `int`

Description: The minute.

Parameter: `iSeconds`

Type: `int`

Description: The second.

Return value: The return value is TRUE if the time is successfully set.

SysSetVolumeName

The `SysSetVolumeName` function sets a disk's volume name.

Syntax: `BOOL  SysSetVolumeName(iDrive,lpszNewVolumeName)`

Parameter: `iDrive`

Type: `int`

Description: The drive (0=current, 1=A, 2=B, and so forth).

Parameter: `lpszNewVolumeName`

Type: `LPSTR`

Description: Pointer to a string containing the new volume name.

Return value: The return value is TRUE if the volume name is set, FALSE if an error occurs.

SysSplitPath

The `SysSplitPath` function splits a drive/path/file string into its component parts.

Syntax:

```
LPSTR  SysSplitPath(lpszPath,lpszDrive,lpszDir,
       lpszFileName,lpszExt)
```

Parameter: `lpszPath`

Type: `LPSTR`

Description: Pointer to the string containing the drive, path, and filename.

Parameter: `lpszDrive`

Type: `LPSTR`

Description: Pointer to a string that receives the drive.

Parameter: `lpszDir`

Type: `LPSTR`

Description: Pointer to a string that receives the directory path.

Parameter: `lpszFileName`

Type: `LPSTR`

Description: Pointer to a string that receives the filename.

Parameter: `lpszExt`

Type: `LPSTR`

Description: Pointer to a string that receives the extension.

Return value: The return value is a pointer to the original path string.

SysValidDrive

The `SysValidDrive` function returns TRUE if the specified drive number represents a valid drive.

Syntax: `BOOL  SysValidDrive(iDrive)`

Parameter: `iDrive`

Type: `int`

Description: The drive to check (0=current, 1=A, 2=B, and so forth).

Return value: The return value is TRUE if the specified drive is valid, FALSE if it isn't.

SysWrite

The `SysWrite` function writes a block of data to an open file.

Syntax: `int SysWrite(iHandle,lpBuffer,uSize,lpWritten)`

Parameter: `iHandle`

Type: `int`

Description: The handle of the file.

Parameter: `lpBuffer`

Type: `LPVOID`

Description: Pointer to the data to be written.

Parameter: `uSize`

Type: `WORD`

Description: The number of bytes to write.

Parameter: `lpWritten`

Type: `LPWORD`

Description: Pointer to the variable that receives the number of bytes actually written.

Return value: The return value is the number of bytes actually written to the file.

SysXCreateFile

The `SysXCreateFile` function creates a file and opens it for writing.

Syntax: `int SysXCreateFile(iAttrib,lpszFilename,lpErrorCode)`

Parameter: `iAttrib`

Type: `int`

Description: The desired attributes for the new file.

Parameter: `lpszFilename`

Type: `LPSTR`

Description: Points to a string containing the filename.

Parameter: `lpErrorCode`

Type: `LPWORD`

Description: Points to a variable that will receive the error code from the operation. Zero indicates successful completion.

Return value: The return value is zero if the function is successful; a nonzero return indicates the file couldn't be created.

WriteFileString

The `WriteFileString` function writes configuration strings to a file.

Syntax: `BOOL WriteFileString(lpszName,lpszTopic,lpszData)`

Parameter: `lpszName`

Type: `LPSTR`

Description: Points to a string containing the filename.

Parameter: `lpszTopic`

Type: `LPSTR`

Description: Points to a string containing the topic name.

Parameter: `lpszData`

Type: `LPSTR`

Description: Points to a string containing the data.

Return value: The return code is TRUE if the operation is successful; FALSE indicates that the file isn't found or can't be written to.

Comments: PowerPack provides the capability to maintain a file of configuration strings. Developers can use it by writing configuration data into it and retrieving the data with the `GetFileString` function. The topic, with an equal sign appended to it, is written to the file, and the data immediately follows.

MISCELLANEOUS FUNCTIONS

The following functions are also included in PowerPack. Some of these functions duplicate or nearly duplicate those in Windows SDK, but all are included here for the sake of completeness.

TABLE 3.8. MISCELLANEOUS FUNCTIONS.

Function	*Description*
`Play`	Plays a song on the PC's speaker.
`PlayChangeSpeed`	Changes the playing speed of the current song.
`PlayFreeze`	Temporarily halts the song currently playing.
`PlayResume`	Resumes playing a halted song.
`PlayStop`	Stops the song currently playing.

PLAY

The `Play` function starts playing a song using the PC's speaker.

Syntax: `HANDLE  Play(hWndParent,lpPlayString,cSpeed)`

Parameter: `hWndParent`

Type: `HWND`

Description: The parent window's handle.

Parameter: `lpPlayString`

Type: `LPSTR`

Description: Points to a string defining the song to play.

Parameter: `cSpeed`

Type: `BYTE`

Description: Specifies the playing speed of the song. Ranges from 0 (slowest) to 9 (fastest).

Return value: The return value is a handle specifying this instance of the play function.

Comments: The string that defines the string to play consists of codes followed by specific data for the codes:

Code	*Meaning*
'A'-'G'	Start playing the specified note. The next characters define the specifics: (Optional) '+' sharps the note (Optional) '-' flats the note Octave designation— '1' (very low) to '9' (very high) (Optional) '/' cuts off the last note before playing this one duration:

Code	*Meaning*
	‘W’ — whole note (4 beats)
	‘H’ — half note (2 beats)
	‘Q’ — quarter note (1 beat)
	‘E’ — eighth note (1/2 beat)
	‘S’ — Sixteenth note (1/4 beat)
	‘T’ — Thirty-second note (1/8 beat)
‘R’	Rest. The remainder of the characters are identical to those for regular notes above.
‘L’	Defines a label, the name of which is the next character.
‘<’	Repeat to a label. The next character is the label’s name. The following character can be ‘1’ through ‘9’, specifying that the repeat should occur from 1 to 9 times, or ‘X’ to indicate an infinite repeat.

The playing of the music occurs in the background, and the developer must ensure that the song is completed (either naturally or through calling).

PlayChangeSpeed

The `PlayChangeSpeed` function changes the play speed of a playing song.

Syntax: `BOOL  PlayChangeSpeed(hPlayInst,cSpeed)`

Parameter: `hPlayInst`

Type: `HANDLE`

Description: The instance handle returned by `Play()`.

Parameter: `cSpeed`

Type: `BYTE`

Description: The new speed (1 through 9).

Return value: The return value is TRUE if `hPlayInst` is valid.

PlayFreeze

The `PlayFreeze` function pauses the currently playing song.

Syntax: `BOOL   PlayFreeze(hPlayInst)`

Parameter: `hPlayInst`

Type: `HANDLE`

Description: The instance handle returned by `Play`.

Return value: The return value is TRUE if `hPlayInst` is valid.

PlayResume

The `PlayResume` function resumes the current song at the point it was frozen.

Syntax: `BOOL   PlayResume(hPlayInst)`

Parameter: `hPlayInst`

Type: `HANDLE`

Description: The instance handle returned by `Play`.

Return value: The return value is TRUE if `hPlayInst` is valid.

PlayStop

The `PlayStop` function stops the currently playing song.

Syntax: `BOOL   PlayStop(hPlayInst)`

Parameter: `hPlayInst`

Type: `HANDLE`

Description: The instance handle returned by `Play`.

Return value: The return value is TRUE if `hPlayInst` is valid.

QUICKSORT

The `QuickSort` function sorts a collection of fixed-length records using the `QuickSort` algorithm.

Syntax: `VOID QuickSort(lpBase,wTotal,wItemWidth,lpfnCompare)`

Parameter: `lpBase`

Type: `LPVOID`

Description: Points to the start of the data to be sorted.

Parameter: `wTotal`

Type: `WORD`

Description: The number of records to be sorted.

Parameter: `wItemWidth`

Type: `WORD`

Description: The width (in bytes) of each record.

Parameter: `lpfnCompare`

Type: `FARPROC`

Description: The procedure instance of the function called to perform the record comparisons.

Return value: The return value is always TRUE.

Comments: The user-supplied function that performs the record comparisons must match the following format:

```
int FAR PASCAL lpCompare(LPVOID pItem1,LPVOID lpItem2);
```

The function should compare the two records and return one of the following values:

<0	if item 1 occurs before item 2.
0	if the items are the same.
>0	if item 2 occurs before item 1.

4

MESSAGE REFERENCE

The following messages are used to communicate with the PowerPack controls. As with Windows-supplied messages, data is passed by the `wParam` and `lParam` function parameters. The **SendMessage** API function should be used to send messages to controls.

EM_GETCARETPOS

The `EM_GETCARETPOS` message is sent to any PowerPack Edit control. The control responds with the current position of the caret.

Parameter: `wParam`

Description: Not used.

Parameter: `lParam`

Description: Not used.

Return value: The current caret position. (0 is the first character position in the field.)

EM_GETFORMAT

The `EM_GETFORMAT` message is sent to a `tbDate` or `tbTime` control. The control responds with its current display format.

Parameter: `wParam`

Description: Not used.

Parameter: `lParam`

Description: Far pointer to a `DATEFORMAT` or `TIMEFORMAT` structure where the current format parameters are placed.

Return value: A nonzero return value indicates success.

EM_SETCARETPOS

The `EM_SETCARETPOS` message is sent to any PowerPack Edit control. The control responds by setting the caret to the specified location in the field.

Parameter: `wParam`

Description: The new caret position.

Parameter: `lParam`

Description: Not used.

Return value: A nonzero return value indicates success.

EM_SETFORMAT

The EM_SETFORMAT message is sent to a tbTime or tbDate control. It specifies the display format for the control.

Parameter: wParam

Description: Not used.

Parameter: lParam

Description: Far pointer to a TIMEFORMAT or DATEFORMAT structure that contains the desired formatting parameters.

Return value: A nonzero return value indicates success.

EM_SETRANGE

The EM_SETRANGE message is sent to a tbFloat, tbInteger, tbTime, or tbDate control. It specifies the range of valid values used by the control.

Parameter: wParam

Description: Not used.

Parameter: lParam

Description: Far pointer to a string that contains the minimum and maximum values separated by a space. For tbDate controls, these values must be specified as Julian dates. For tbTime controls, they must be specified as seconds past midnight.

Return value: A nonzero return value indicates success.

IM_GETCOLOR

The IM_GETCOLOR message is sent to a tbImprint control. It retrieves the colors used when drawing the control.

Parameter: wParam

Description: Not used.

Parameter: lParam

Description: A far pointer to an IMPRINTCOLOR structure that retrieves the colors to use.

Return value: None.

IM_GETFRAMESIZE

The IM_GETFRAMESIZE message is sent to a tbImprint control. The control responds with the width of the frame in pixels. Frames are specified by the IS_FRAME_IN or IS_FRAME_OUT styles.

Parameter: wParam

Description: Not used.

Parameter: lParam

Description: Not used.

Return value: The size of the frame in pixels.

IM_GETLINECNT

The IM_GETLINECNT message is sent to a tbImprint control. The control responds with the number of horizontal and vertical lines of text it contains.

Parameter: wParam

Description: Not used.

Parameter: lParam

Description: Not used.

Return value: The low word contains the number of horizontal lines, and the high word contains the number of vertical lines.

IM_GETLINESIZE

The `IM_GETLINESIZE` message is sent to a `tbImprint` control. The control responds with the width of the lines.

Parameter: `wParam`

Description: Not used.

Parameter: `lParam`

Description: Not used.

Return value: The width of the lines in pixels.

IM_GETSHADOWSIZE

The `IM_GETSHADOWSIZE` message is sent to a `tbImprint` control. The control responds with the width of the shadow placed around it.

Parameter: `wParam`

Description: Not used.

Parameter: `lParam`

Description: Not used.

Return value: The width of the shadow in pixels.

IM_SETCOLOR

The `IM_SETCOLOR` message is sent to a `tbImprint` control. It specifies the colors used to draw the control.

Parameter: `wParam`

Description: Not used.

Parameter: `lParam`

Description: A far pointer to an `IMPRINTCOLOR` structure that defines the colors to use.

Return value: None.

IM_SETFRAMESIZE

The IM_SETFRAMESIZE message is sent to a tbImprint control. It specifies the size of the frame inside the Imprint control. Frames are specified using the IS_FRAME_OUT or IS_FRAME_IN style flags. The default size for a frame is three pixels.

Parameter: wParam

Description: The size of the frame in pixels.

Parameter: lParam

Description: Not used.

Return value: None.

IM_SETLINECNT

The IM_SETLINECNT message is sent to a tbImprint control. It specifies the number of horizontal and vertical lines displayed in the control. This is very useful when displaying data in tabular form.

Parameter: wParam

Description: Not used.

Parameter: lParam

Description: The low word specifies the number of horizontal lines, and the high word specifies the number of vertical lines.

Return value: None.

IM_SETLINESIZE

The IM_SETLINESIZE message is sent to a tbImprint control. It specifies the width of the lines drawn in the control.

Parameter: wParam

Description: The size of the line in pixels.

Parameter: lParam

Description: Not used.

Return value: None.

IM_SETSHADOWSIZE

The IM_SETSHADOWSIZE message is sent to a tbImprint control. It specifies the width of the shadow displayed around the control.

Parameter: wParam

Description: The width of the shadow in pixels.

Parameter: lParam

Description: Not used.

Return value: None.

PM_GETPOS

The PM_GETPOS message is sent to a tbProgress control. The control responds with its current position.

Parameter: wParam

Description: Not used.

Parameter: lParam

Description: Not used.

Return value: The current position of the tbProgress control progress bar.

PM_GETRANGE

The `PM_GETRANGE` message is sent to a `tbProgress` control. The control responds with its configured range.

Parameter: `wParam`

Description: Not used.

Parameter: `lParam`

Description: Not used.

Return value: The low word of the return value specifies the minimum value. The high word of the return value specifies the maximum value.

PM_SETPOS

The `PM_SETPOS` message is sent to a `tbProgress` control. It specifies a new position for the progress bar.

Parameter: `wParam`

Description: The new position for the progress bar.

Parameter: `lParam`

Description: Not used.

Return value: None.

Comments: The value must fall within the configured range of the progress bar; if not, it is ignored.

PM_SETRANGE

The `PM_SETRANGE` message is sent to a `tbProgress` control. It specifies the minimum and maximum values for the progress bar.

Parameter: `wParam`

Description: Not used.

Parameter: `lParam`

Description: The low word is the minimum value. The high word is the maximum value.

Return value: None.

VPM_CLEAR

The `VPM_CLEAR` message is sent to a `tbViewPict` control. The picture associated with the control is cleared (erased).

Parameter: `wParam`

Description: Not used.

Parameter: `lParam`

Description: Not used.

Return value: None.

VPM_FREEZEANIMATION

The `VPM_FREEZEANIMATION` message is sent to a `tbViewPict` control. If animation is occurring, it freezes at the current frame.

Parameter: `wParam`

Description: Not used.

Parameter: `lParam`

Description: Not used.

Return value: None.

VPM_SETFRAMES

The `VPM_SETFRAMES` message is sent to a `tbViewPict` control. It specifies a series of frames and describes how they are to be displayed.

Parameter: `wParam`

Description: Not used.

Parameter: `lParam`

Description: Far pointer to a `VIEWPICT_ANIMATE` structure, which specifies the frames and the display information.

Return value: One of the following values:

> `VIEWPICT_ERR_OK` (no error).
> `VIEWPICT_ERR_NOTFOUND` (one or more pictures not found).
> `VIEWPICT_ERR_MEMORY` (insufficient memory).
> `VIEWPICT_ERR_FILEERR` (picture file corrupt).
> `VIEWPICT_ERR_BADPICT` (unknown picture format).

VPM_SETPICTURE

The `VPM_SETPICTURE` message is sent to a `tbViewPict` control. It specifies the single picture to be displayed by the control.

Parameter: `wParam`

Description: The style bits for the control.

Parameter: `lParam`

Description: The resource or filename of the picture.

Return value: One of the following values:

> `VIEWPICT_ERR_OK` (no error).
> `VIEWPICT_ERR_NOTFOUND` (one or more pictures not found).
> `VIEWPICT_ERR_MEMORY` (insufficient memory).
> `VIEWPICT_ERR_FILEERR` (picture file corrupt).
> `VIEWPICT_ERR_BADPICT` (unknown picture format).

VPM_SETSTYLE

The VPM_SETSTYLE message is sent to a tbViewPict control. It specifies a new style for the control.

Parameter: wParam

Description: Not used.

Parameter: lParam

Description: The new control style.

Return value: None.

VPM_SHOWNEXTFRAME

The VPM_SHOWNEXTFRAME message is sent to a tbViewPict control in which animation is being used. The control displays the next frame in the animation sequence. If the last frame is reached, the first frame in the series is displayed.

Parameter: wParam

Description: Not used.

Parameter: lParam

Description: Not used.

Return value: None.

VPM_SHOWPREVFRAME

The VPM_SHOWPREVFRAME message is sent to a tbViewPict control in which animation is being used. The control displays the previous frame in the animation sequence. If the first frame is reached, the last frame in the series is displayed.

Parameter: wParam

Description: Not used.

Parameter: `lParam`

Description: Not used.

Return value: None.

VPM_STARTANIMATION

The `VPM_STARTANIMATION` message is sent to a `tbViewPict` control in which animation is being used. The control begins animating the frames.

Parameter: `wParam`

Description: Not used.

Parameter: `lParam`

Description: Not used.

Return value: None.

VPN_KILLFOCUS

The `VPN_KILLFOCUS` notification is sent to the parent of a `tbViewPict` control when the control loses input focus. The parent receives the communication through a `WM_COMMAND` message from the control.

Parameter: `wParam`

Description: The control ID of the `tbViewPict` control.

Parameter: `lParam`

Description: Low word: the window handle of the `tbViewPict` control. High word: `VPN_KILLFOCUS`.

Return value: None.

VPN_SETFOCUS

The `VPN_SETFOCUS` notification is sent to the parent of a `tbViewPict` control when the control receives input focus. The parent receives the communication through a WM_COMMAND message from the control.

Parameter: wParam

Description: The control ID of the tbViewPict control.

Parameter: lParam

Description: Low word: the window handle of the tbViewPict control. High word: VPN_SETFOCUS.

Return value: None.

VTM_ADDSTRING

The VTM_ADDSTRING message is sent to a tbViewText control. It adds a string to the end of the control's text and updates the display.

Parameter: wParam

Description: Not used.

Parameter: lParam

Description: Far pointer to the string to be added.

Return value: None.

VTM_CLEAR

The VTM_CLEAR message is sent to a tbViewText control. It clears (removes) all the text in the control.

Parameter: wParam

Description: Not used.

Parameter: lParam

Description: Not used.

Return value: None.

VTM_DELETESTRING

The VTM_DELETESTRING message is sent to a tbViewText control. It deletes a string from the control and updates the display.

Parameter: wParam

Description: Index of the string to be deleted.

Parameter: lParam

Description: Not used.

Return value: None.

VTM_GETCOLOR

The VTM_GETCOLOR message is sent to a tbViewText control. The control responds with a structure that contains all the colors used to draw the control.

Parameter: wParam

Description: Not used.

Parameter: lParam

Description: Far pointer to a VIEWTEXTCOLOR structure.

Return value: None.

VTM_GETLINECOUNT

The VTM_GETLINECOUNT message is sent to a tbViewText control. The control responds with the total number of text lines contained in the control.

Parameter: wParam

Description: Not used.

Parameter: lParam

Description: Not used.

Return value: The number of text lines.

VTM_GETSTRING

The `VTM_GETSTRING` message is sent to a `tbViewText` control. A specified line of text is copied from the control to the specified string.

Parameter: `wParam`

Description: The index of the line to retrieve.

Parameter: `lParam`

Description: Far pointer to the destination string.

Return value: None.

VTM_GETSTRINGLEN

The `VTM_GETSTRINGLEN` message is sent to a `tbViewText` control. The control responds with the number of characters contained in a given line of text in the control.

Parameter: `wParam`

Description: The index of the string.

Parameter: `lParam`

Description: Not used.

Return value: The length of the specified string.

VTM_GETTOPINDEX

The `VTM_GETTOPINDEX` message is sent to a `tbViewText` control. The control responds with the index of the text line currently displayed at the top of the control.

Parameter: `wParam`

Description: Not used.

Parameter: `lParam`

Description: Not used.

Return value: The index of the top line.

VTM_HIGHLIGHTTEXT

The `VTM_HIGHLIGHTTEXT` message is sent to a `tbViewText` control. It causes all or part of a specified string to be highlighted.

Parameter: `wParam`

Description: The index of the string in the control.

Parameter: `lParam`

Description: Low word: the column position where highlighting begins. High word: the number of characters to highlight.

Return value: None.

VTM_INSERTSTRING

The `VTM_INSERTSTRING` message is sent to the `tbViewText` control. The specified string is inserted into the control's text at the specified line number.

Parameter: `wParam`

Description: The line number where the string is placed.

Parameter: `lParam`

Description: Far pointer to the string to be inserted.

Return value: None.

VTM_REDRAW

The `VTM_REDRAW` message is sent to a `tbViewText` control. The control is redrawn.

Parameter: `wParam`

Description: Not used.

Parameter: `lParam`

Description: Not used.

Return value: None.

Comments: Adding or inserting data into the control doesn't cause an immediate redraw. The application must cause the redraw to occur at the proper times through this message.

VTM_RETRIEVETEXT

If a `tbViewText` control is assigned the style `VS_OWNERSUPPLYTEXT`, the `VTM_RETRIEVETEXT` message is sent to the parent of the control. This is a request from the control for another line of text.

Parameter: `wParam`

Description: Not used.

Parameter: `lParam`

Description: Far pointer to a `VIEWRETRIEVETEXT` structure, which defines the text needed by the control.

Return value: None.

VTM_SEARCH

The `VTM_SEARCH` message is sent to a `tbViewText` control. It requests a search for a substring in all text contained in the control.

Parameter: `wParam`

Description: The methodology of the search (specify only one from each of the following groups and OR them together):

(Case sensitivity)

```
VIEWTEXT_SEARCH_CASE
VIEWTEXT_SEARCH_NOCASE
```

(Where to start search)

```
VIEWTEXT_SEARCH_CURRENT
VIEWTEXT_SEARCH_BEGIN
VIEWTEXT_SEARCH_END
```

(The direction to search)

```
VIEWTEXT_SEARCH_FORWARD
VIEWTEXT_SEARCH_BACKWARD
```

(Match substring or whole word only)

```
VIEWTEXT_SEARCH_SUBSTRING
VIEWTEXT_SEARCH_WHOLEWORD
```

Parameter: `lParam`

Description: Far pointer to a string that contains the text for which to search.

Return value: The result is TRUE if text is found, FALSE if not.

VTM_SEARCHREPEAT

The `VTM_SEARCHREPEAT` message is sent to a `tbViewText` control. It repeats the last search from the point of the last occurrence of the text.

Parameter: `wParam`

Description: Not used.

Parameter: `lParam`

Description: Not used.

Return value: The result is TRUE if text is found, FALSE if not.

VTM_SETCOLHEADERS

The `VTM_SETCOLHEADERS` message is sent to a `tbViewText` control. It defines the number of rows to lock as column headers at the top of the control. These rows don't scroll vertically but do scroll horizontally.

Parameter: wParam

Description: The number of rows to lock as column headers.

Parameter: lParam

Description: Not used.

Return value: None.

VTM_SETCOLOR

The VTM_SETCOLOR message is sent to a tbViewText control. It defines the colors used to draw the various parts of the control.

Parameter: wParam

Description: Not used.

Parameter: lParam

Description: Far pointer to a VIEWTEXTCOLOR structure.

Return value: None.

VTM_SETHEADER

The VTM_SETHEADER message is sent to a tbViewText control. It defines the number of lines to lock as the document header at the top of the screen. These lines always appear at the top and can't scroll in any direction.

Parameter: wParam

Description: The number of header lines.

Parameter: lParam

Description: Not used.

Return value: None.

VTM_SETROWHEADERS

The `VTM_SETROWHEADERS` message is sent to a `tbViewText` control. It defines the number of left-hand columns to lock as row headers. These columns always appear on the screen and can't be scrolled horizontally.

Parameter: `wParam`

Description: The number of columns to lock.

Parameter: `lParam`

Description: Not used.

Return value: None.

VTM_SETTOPINDEX

The `VTM_SETTOPINDEX` message is sent to a `tbViewText` control. The control scrolls its text so that the specified line appears at the top of the control.

Parameter: `wParam`

Description: The index of the line displayed at the top.

Parameter: `lParam`

Description: Not used.

Return value: None.

VTM_VIEWSIZE

If a `tbViewText` control is assigned the style `VS_OWNERSUPPLYTEXT`, the `VTM_VIEWSIZE` message is sent to the control's parent. The parent fills in the `Max` and `ItemCnt` members of the structure, so the control knows the amount of text it is to handle at a time.

Parameter: `wParam`

Description: Not used.

Parameter: `lParam`

Description: Far pointer to a `VIEWSIZE` structure, which is filled in by the parent.

Return value: None.

VTN_KILLFOCUS

The `VTN_KILLFOCUS` notification is sent to the parent of a `tbViewText` control when the control loses input focus. The parent receives the message through a `WM_COMMAND` message from the control.

Parameter: `wParam`

Description: The control ID of the `tbViewText` control.

Parameter: `lParam`

Description: Low word: the window handle of the `tbViewText` control. High word: `VTN_KILLFOCUS`.

Return value: None.

VTN_SETFOCUS

The `VTN_SETFOCUS` notification is sent to the parent of a `tbViewText` control when the control receives input focus. The parent receives the information through a `WM_COMMAND` message from the control.

Parameter: `wParam`

Description: The control ID of the `tbViewText` control.

Parameter: `lParam`

Description: Low word: the window handle of the `tbViewText` control. High word: `VTN_SETFOCUS`.

Return value: None.

5

STRUCTURE REFERENCE

The following structures are defined in powerpak.h and are needed to pass information to the various functions and controls described in this document.

DATE

```
typedef struct tagDATE
   {
   int  nDay;        // Day of the Month  1..31
   int  nMonth;      // Month of the Year 1..12
   int  nYear;       // Year
   } DATE, FAR *LPDATE;
```

DATEFORMAT

```
typedef struct tagDATEFORMAT
   {
   BOOL   bCentury;      // Should year be displayed as
                         // century
   char   cSeparator;    // Character to use as date
                         // separator
   int    nFormat;       // Date format
   } DATEFORMAT, FAR *LPDATEFORMAT;
```

DISKINFO

```
typedef struct tagDISKINFO
   {
   WORD  bytesPerSector;       // Bytes in a Sector
                               // (normally 512)
   WORD  clustersPerDrive;     // Clusters per Device
   WORD  sectorsPerCluster;    // Sectors in a Cluster
   WORD  availableClusters;    // Number of free Clusters
   } DISKINFO, FAR *LPDISKINFO;
```

FILEINFO

```
typedef struct tagFILEINFO
   {
   char  reserved[ 21];       // Reserved for next
                              // SysFindNext
   char  attrib;              // Attribute of this file
   int   time;                // Time of last modification
   int   date;                // Date of last modification
   LONG  fileSize;            // Size of file
   char  fileName[ 13];       // File name
   } FILEINFO, FAR *LPFILEINFO;
```

FLOATFORMAT

```
typedef struct tagFLOATFORMAT
   {
   char   cCurrencySign;     // Currency symbol
   char   cDecimalSign;      // Character for decimal pt
   char   cSeparator;        // Thousand separator char
   } FLOATFORMAT, FAR *LPFLOATFORMAT;
```

IMPRINTCOLOR

```
typedef struct imprintcolor
   {
   COLORREF Color;               // Background color
   COLORREF ColorFrame;          // Color of frame
   COLORREF ColorShadow;         // Color of shadow
   COLORREF ColorHighlight;      // Color of highlight
   COLORREF ColorInsideBorder;   // Color of inside border
   COLORREF ColorOutsideBorder;// Color of outside
                                 // border
   COLORREF ColorText;           // Text color
   COLORREF ColorLines;          // Color of lines
   } IMPRINTCOLOR, FAR *LPIMPRINT
```

TIME

```
typedef struct tagTIME
   {
   int  nHour;      // Hour 0..23
   int  nMinute;    // Minutes 0..59
   int  nSecond;    // Seconds 0..59
   } TIME, FAR *LPTIME;
```

TIMEFORMAT

```
typedef struct tagTIMEFORMAT
   {
   BOOL   b24Hour;     // Should military time be
                       // displayed
   BOOL   bSeconds;    // Should seconds be displayed
   char   cSeparator;  // Separator character to be used
   } TIMEFORMAT, FAR *LPTIMEFORMAT;
```

VIEWPICT_ANIMATE

```
typedef struct viewpict_animate
   {
   VIEWPICT_ANIMATEHDR    AnimateHdr;    // Header
                                         // information
   LPVIEWPICT_ANIMATEPICT AnimatePict;   // Pointer to an
                                         // array
                                         // of Picture
                                         // structures
   } VIEWPICT_ANIMATE, FAR *LPVIEWPICT_ANIMATE;
```

VIEWPICT_ANIMATEHDR

```
typedef struct viewpict_animatehdr
   {
   short PictureCnt;      // The total number of frames
   short TimeDelay;       // The default delay between
                          // frames (ms)
   } VIEWPICT_ANIMATEHDR, FAR *LPVIEWPICT_ANIMATEHDR;
```

VIEWPICT_ANIMATEPICT

```
typedef struct viewpict_animatepict
   {
   LPSTR PictName;          // The filename or resource ID
   short PictStyle;         // The style bits for the
                            // picture
   short x;                 // Starting position x coord
   short y;                 // Starting position y coord
   short TimeDelay;         // Time to display this frame
                            // (ms)
   } VIEWPICT_ANIMATEPICT, FAR *LPVIEWPICT_ANIMATEPICT;
```

VIEWSIZE

```
typedef struct viewsize
   {
   short WidthMax;        // Maximum width of the text
   short ItemCnt;         // Total lines of text
   } VIEWSIZE, FAR *LPVIEWSIZE;
```

VIEWRETRIEVETEXT

```
typedef struct viewretrievetext
   {
   short ItemNum;         // Line number being requested
   LPSTR ItemText;        // Text is placed here
   } VIEWRETRIEVETEXT, FAR *LPVIEWRETRIEVETEXT;
```

VIEWTEXTCOLOR

```
typedef struct viewtextcolor
   {
   COLORREF BackGround;    // Background color
   COLORREF MainText;      // Color of main text
   COLORREF Header;        // Color of header
   COLORREF ColTitles;     // Color of column titles
   COLORREF RowTitles;     // Color of row titles
   COLORREF HighLightText; // Color of highlighted text
   COLORREF HighLightBk;   // Highlighted text back-
                           // ground color
   } VIEWTEXTCOLOR, FAR *LPVIEWTEXTCOLOR;
```

WINDEVICE

```
typedef struct tagWINDEVICE
   {
   char DeviceName[50];
   char DriverName[9];
   char Port[40];
   } WINDEVICE;
```

A

Source Code Listings

This appendix provides the source code listing of the example program on the companion diskette.

Listing A.1. The makefile (POWER).

```
CC = cl -c -AM -Gsw -Od -W3 -Zpi -Fo$@

all: power.exe

power.h: dialog.h resource.h

power.res: power.rc power.dlg dialog.h resource.h
  rc -r power
```

continues

LISTING A.1. CONTINUED

```
about.obj: about.c power.h
  $(CC) $*.c

datetime.obj: datetime.c power.h
  $(CC) $*.c

filecopy.obj: filecopy.c power.h
  $(CC) $*.c

floatint.obj: floatint.c power.h
  $(CC) $*.c

imprint.obj: imprint.c power.h
  $(CC) $*.c

init.obj: init.c power.h
  $(CC) $*.c

play.obj: play.c power.h
  $(CC) $*.c

power.obj: power.c power.h
  $(CC) $*.c

progress.obj: progress.c power.h
  $(CC) $*.c

sysfunc.obj: sysfunc.c power.h
  $(CC) $*.c

travel.obj: travel.c power.h
  $(CC) $*.c

view.obj: view.c power.h
  $(CC) $*.c

winmain.obj: winmain.c power.h
  $(CC) $*.c

power.exe:: about.obj datetime.obj filecopy.obj \
            floatint.obj imprint.obj init.obj \
            play.obj power.obj progress.obj sysfunc.obj \
            travel.obj view.obj winmain.obj \
            power.res power.def
    link /CO /MAP /NOD @<<
```

```
about+
datetime+
filecopy+
floatint+
imprint+
init+
play+
power+
progress+
sysfunc+
travel+
view+
winmain
$@

libw mlibcew powerpak
power.def
<<
    mapsym power
    rc power.res
```

Listing A.2. Dialog definition file (POWER.DLG).

```
DLGINCLUDE RCDATA DISCARDABLE
BEGIN
    "DIALOG.H\0"
END

ID_IMPRINT DIALOG 0, 0, 280, 182
STYLE DS_MODALFRAME ¦ WS_POPUP ¦ WS_VISIBLE ¦ WS_CAPTION
    ¦ WS_SYSMENU
CAPTION "Imprint Demo"
BEGIN
    CONTROL         "Imprint Example ""Out""",
                    IDD_IMPRINT_OUT,
                    "tbImprint", 0x2201, 8, 10, 120, 20
    CONTROL         "Imprint Example ""In""",
                    IDD_IMPRINT_IN,
                    "tbImprint", 0x2202, 8, 40, 120, 20
    CONTROL         "Group Box", IDD_IMPRINT_GROUPBOX,
                    "tbImprint",
                    0x42C2, 8, 70, 120, 20
```

continues

LISTING A.2. CONTINUED

```
    CONTROL          "Imprint Example ""Out"" with
                     Frame",
                     IDD_IMPRINT_OUTFRAME, "tbImprint",
                     0x2205, 8, 100, 120,
                     20
    CONTROL          "Imprint Example ""Out"" with
                     Frame",
                     IDD_PROGRESS_VPROGRESS, "tbImprint",
                     0x2209, 140, 100,
                     120, 20
    CONTROL          "Imprint Example ""In"" with Frame",
                     IDD_IMPRINT_INFRAME, "tbImprint",
                     0x2206, 8, 130,
                     120, 20
    CONTROL          "Imprint Example ""In"" with Frame",
                     IDD_IMPRINT_LINESIN, "tbImprint",
                     0x220A, 140,
                     130, 120, 20
    CONTROL          "", IDD_IMPRINT_LINESOUT,
                     "tbImprint", 0x0002,
                     140, 10, 120, 39
    CTEXT            "Text 1", 0, 142, 13, 25, 8, NOT
                     WS_GROUP
    CTEXT            "Text 2", 0, 172, 13, 25, 8, NOT
                     WS_GROUP
    CTEXT            "Text 3", 0, 202, 13, 25, 8, NOT
                     WS_GROUP
    CTEXT            "Text 4", 0, 232, 13, 25, 8, NOT
                     WS_GROUP
    CTEXT            "Text 5", 0, 142, 26, 25, 8, NOT
                     WS_GROUP
    CTEXT            "Text 6", 0, 172, 26, 25, 8, NOT
                     WS_GROUP
    CTEXT            "Text 7", 0, 202, 26, 25, 8, NOT
                     WS_GROUP
    CTEXT            "Text 8", 0, 232, 26, 25, 8, NOT
                     WS_GROUP
    CTEXT            "Text 9", 0, 142, 39, 25, 8, NOT
                     WS_GROUP
    CTEXT            "Text 10", 0, 172, 39, 25, 8, NOT
                     WS_GROUP
    CTEXT            "Text 11", 0, 202, 39, 25, 8, NOT
                     WS_GROUP
    CTEXT            "Text 12", 0, 232, 39, 25, 8, NOT
                     WS_GROUP
```

```
    CONTROL             "", IDD_IMPRINT_OK, "tbImprint",
                        0x0001, 140, 54, 120,
                        39
    CTEXT               "Text 1", 0, 142, 57, 25, 8, NOT
                        WS_GROUP
    CTEXT               "Text 2", 0, 172, 57, 25, 8, NOT
                        WS_GROUP
    CTEXT               "Text 3", 0, 202, 57, 25, 8, NOT
                        WS_GROUP
    CTEXT               "Text 4", 0, 232, 57, 25, 8, NOT
                        WS_GROUP
    CTEXT               "Text 5", 0, 142, 70, 25, 8, NOT
                        WS_GROUP
    CTEXT               "Text 6", 0, 172, 70, 25, 8, NOT
                        WS_GROUP
    CTEXT               "Text 7", 0, 202, 70, 25, 8, NOT
                        WS_GROUP
    CTEXT               "Text 8", 0, 232, 70, 25, 8, NOT
                        WS_GROUP
    CTEXT               "Text 9", 0, 142, 83, 25, 8, NOT
                        WS_GROUP
    CTEXT               "Text 10", 0, 172, 83, 25, 8, NOT
                        WS_GROUP
    CTEXT               "Text 11", 0, 202, 83, 25, 8, NOT
                        WS_GROUP
    CTEXT               "Text 12", 0, 232, 83, 25, 8, NOT
                        WS_GROUP
    DEFPUSHBUTTON       "OK", IDOK, 126, 160, 28, 14,
                        WS_GROUP
END

ID_PROGRESS DIALOG 80, 37, 156, 90
STYLE DS_MODALFRAME ¦ WS_POPUP ¦ WS_VISIBLE ¦ WS_CAPTION
    ¦ WS_SYSMENU
CAPTION "Progress Demo"
BEGIN
    CONTROL             "", IDD_PROGRESS_HPROGRESS,
                        "tbProgress", WS_BORDER ¦
                        0x0002, 8, 20, 80, 12
    PUSHBUTTON          "<-", IDD_PROGRESS_HPROGRESSLEFT, 8,
                        36, 28, 14
    PUSHBUTTON          "->", IDD_PROGRESS_HPROGRESSRIGHT,
                        60, 36, 28, 14
    CONTROL             "", IDD_PROGRESS_VPROGRESS,
                        "tbProgress", WS_BORDER ¦
                        0x0005, 100, 10, 16, 50
```

continues

LISTING A.2. CONTINUED

```
    PUSHBUTTON        "->", IDD_PROGRESS_VPROGRESSRIGHT,
                      120, 17, 28, 14
    PUSHBUTTON        "<-", IDD_PROGRESS_VPROGRESSLEFT,
                      120, 38, 28, 14
    DEFPUSHBUTTON     "OK", IDOK, 62, 72, 40, 14
END

ID_ABOUTBOX DIALOG 25, 21, 184, 160
STYLE DS_MODALFRAME ¦ WS_POPUP ¦ WS_CAPTION ¦ WS_SYSMENU
CAPTION "About Windows Programmer's Power Pack"
BEGIN
    CONTROL           "", 0, "tbImprint", 0x0001, 8, 6,
                      167, 56
    CTEXT             "Windows Programmer's", 0, 47, 9,
                      92, 8
    CTEXT             "Power Pack", 0, 54, 18, 72, 8
    CONTROL           "", 0, "tbImprint", 0x0001, 8, 65,
                      168, 72
    CONTROL           "", IDD_ABOUT_LOGO, "tbViewPict",
                      0x0001, 17,
                      67, 150, 40
    CTEXT             "Copyright _ 1991, 1992 FarPoint
                      Technologies", 0, 10,
                      111, 164, 8
    CTEXT             "PO Box 309  Richmond, Oh  43944",
                      0, 10, 119, 164, 8
    CTEXT             "Phone (614) 765-4333    Fax (614)
                      765-4939", 0, 10, 127,
                      164, 8
    DEFPUSHBUTTON     "OK", IDOK, 74, 143, 36, 14,
                      WS_GROUP
    LTEXT             "Based on ", 134, 77, 33, 36, 8
    LTEXT             "Drover's Professional Toolbox for
                      Windows", 135, 22, 42,
                      146, 8
    LTEXT             "From", 136, 83, 53, 18, 8
END

ID_SYSFUNCS DIALOG 41, 45, 230, 66
STYLE WS_POPUP ¦ WS_CAPTION
CAPTION "Doslib Functions Demo"
BEGIN
    RTEXT             "Number of Drives:", -1, 0, 3, 80,
                      12, NOT WS_GROUP
```

```
    LTEXT           "", IDD_NODRIVES, 82, 3, 20, 12, NOT
                    WS_GROUP
    RTEXT           "Fixed:", -1, 100, 3, 40, 12, NOT
                    WS_GROUP
    LTEXT           "", IDD_FIXEDDRIVES, 142, 3, 20, 12,
                    NOT WS_GROUP
    RTEXT           "Network:", -1, 160, 3, 40, 12, NOT
                    WS_GROUP
    LTEXT           "", IDD_NETWORKDRIVES, 202, 3, 20,
                    12, NOT WS_GROUP
    CONTROL         "Black Line", -1, "Static",
                    SS_BLACKRECT, 0, 16, 250, 1
    RTEXT           "Current Drive:", -1, 0, 20, 66, 12,
                    NOT WS_GROUP
    LTEXT           "", IDD_CURRENTDRIVE, 68, 20, 20,
                    12, NOT WS_GROUP
    RTEXT           "Total Disk Space:", -1, 84, 20, 70,
                    12, NOT WS_GROUP
    LTEXT           "", IDD_TOTALSPACE, 156, 20, 100,
                    12, NOT WS_GROUP
    RTEXT           "Space Free:", -1, 84, 34, 70, 12,
                    NOT WS_GROUP
    LTEXT           "", IDD_FREESPACE, 156, 34, 100, 12,
                    NOT WS_GROUP
    RTEXT           "", IDD_PERCENTFULL, 134, 48, 20,
                    12, NOT WS_GROUP
    LTEXT           "% Full", -1, 156, 48, 30, 12, NOT
                    WS_GROUP
    DEFPUSHBUTTON   "OK", IDOK, 30, 42, 30, 14
END

ID_FILECOPY DIALOG 85, 41, 145, 78
STYLE WS_POPUP ¦ WS_CAPTION
CAPTION "File Copy"
BEGIN
    RTEXT           "From:", -1, 3, 14, 20, 8, NOT
                    WS_GROUP
    EDITTEXT        IDD_FILECOPYSRC, 28, 12, 113, 12,
                    ES_AUTOHSCROLL
    RTEXT           "To:", -1, 7, 32, 16, 8, NOT
                    WS_GROUP
    EDITTEXT        IDD_FILECOPYDST, 28, 30, 113, 12,
                    ES_AUTOHSCROLL
    PUSHBUTTON      "&Copy", IDD_FILECOPY, 23, 59, 41,
                    14
```

continues

LISTING A.2. CONTINUED

```
    PUSHBUTTON      "E&xit", IDCANCEL, 87, 60, 41, 14
END

ID_TRAVEL DIALOG 17, 11, 250, 157
STYLE WS_POPUP ¦ WS_CAPTION
CAPTION "Travel Expenses"
BEGIN
    LTEXT           "EXPENSES FOR THE CURRENT PERIOD",
                    -1, 61, 6, 135, 9,
                    NOT WS_GROUP
    CONTROL         "", IDD_STARTDATE, "tbdate",
                    WS_TABSTOP ¦ 0x2000, 75, 29,
                    50, 10
    CONTROL         "", 0, "tbImprint", 0x0002, 74, 28,
                    52, 12
    CONTROL         "", IDD_ENDDATE, "tbdate",
                    WS_TABSTOP ¦ 0x2000, 149, 29,
                    50, 10
    CONTROL         "", 0, "tbImprint", 0x0002, 148, 28,
                    52, 12
    CONTROL         "9999999.99", IDD_VAL1, "tbfloat",
                    WS_TABSTOP ¦ 0x3000,
                    79, 65, 50, 10
    CONTROL         "", 0, "tbImprint", 0x0002, 78, 64,
                    52, 12
    CONTROL         "9999999.99", IDD_VAL2, "tbfloat",
                    WS_TABSTOP ¦ 0x3000,
                    79, 79, 50, 10
    CONTROL         "", 0, "tbImprint", 0x0002, 78, 78,
                    52, 12
    CONTROL         "9999999.99", IDD_VAL3, "tbfloat",
                    WS_TABSTOP ¦ 0x3000,
                    79, 93, 50, 10
    CONTROL         "", 0, "tbImprint", 0x0002, 78, 92,
                    52, 12
    CONTROL         "9999999.99", IDD_VAL4, "tbfloat",
                    WS_TABSTOP ¦ 0x3000,
                    79, 107, 50, 10
    CONTROL         "", 0, "tbImprint", 0x0002, 78, 106,
                    52, 12
    CONTROL         "9999999.99", IDD_VAL5, "tbfloat",
                    WS_TABSTOP ¦ 0x3200,
                    161, 107, 58, 10
```

```
    CONTROL         "", 0, "tbImprint", 0x0002, 160,
                    106, 60, 12
    LTEXT           "From:", -1, 52, 29, 20, 8, NOT
                    WS_GROUP
    LTEXT           "To:", -1, 134, 29, 13, 8, NOT
                    WS_GROUP
    RTEXT           "Accommodation:", -1, 26, 66, 49,
                    11, NOT WS_GROUP
    RTEXT           "Car:", -1, 29, 80, 46, 10, NOT
                    WS_GROUP
    RTEXT           "Entertainment:", -1, 28, 94, 47,
                    10, NOT WS_GROUP
    RTEXT           "Other:", -1, 38, 108, 37, 10, NOT
                    WS_GROUP
    LTEXT           "Total:", -1, 134, 108, 20, 10, NOT
                    WS_GROUP
    CONTROL         "", 0, "tbImprint", 0x0003, 22, 55,
                    209, 71
    DEFPUSHBUTTON   "OK", IDOK, 54, 137, 44, 14
    PUSHBUTTON      "Cancel", IDCANCEL, 152, 137, 44, 14
END

ID_DATETIME DIALOG 22, 10, 286, 144
STYLE WS_POPUP ¦ WS_CAPTION
CAPTION "Date / Calendar and Time Example"
BEGIN
    LTEXT           "DS_DDMONYY", -1, 15, 26, 52, 8, NOT
                    WS_GROUP
    LTEXT           "DS_CENTURY", -1, 15, 42, 52, 8, NOT
                    WS_GROUP
    LTEXT           "DS_MMDDYY", -1, 15, 58, 52, 8, NOT
                    WS_GROUP
    LTEXT           "DS_YYMMDD", -1, 15, 74, 52, 8, NOT
                    WS_GROUP
    LTEXT           "DS_DDMMYY", -1, 15, 90, 52, 10, NOT
                    WS_GROUP
    CONTROL         "", IDD_DATE1, "tbdate", WS_BORDER ¦
                    WS_TABSTOP ¦ 0x2040,
                    73, 24, 52, 12
    CONTROL         "", IDD_DATE2, "tbdate", WS_BORDER ¦
                    WS_TABSTOP ¦ 0x3040,
                    73, 40, 52, 12
    CONTROL         "", IDD_DATE3, "tbdate", WS_BORDER ¦
                    WS_TABSTOP ¦ 0x6040,
                    73, 56, 52, 12
```

continues

LISTING A.2. CONTINUED

```
    CONTROL          "", IDD_DATE4, "tbdate", WS_BORDER ¦
                     WS_TABSTOP ¦ 0x9040,
                     73, 72, 52, 12
    CONTROL          "", IDD_DATE5, "tbdate", WS_BORDER ¦
                     WS_TABSTOP ¦ 0x4000,
                     73, 88, 52, 12
    LTEXT            "TS_12HOUR", -1, 156, 26, 52, 8, NOT
                     WS_GROUP
    LTEXT            "TS_12HOUR ¦ TS_SECONDS", -1, 156,
                     42, 52, 17, NOT
                     WS_GROUP
    LTEXT            "TS_24HOUR", -1, 156, 66, 52, 8, NOT
                     WS_GROUP
    LTEXT            "TS_24HOUR ¦ TS_SECONDS", -1, 156,
                     82, 52, 19, NOT
                     WS_GROUP
    CONTROL          "", IDD_TIME1, "tbtime", WS_BORDER ¦
                     WS_TABSTOP ¦ 0x9000,
                     217, 24, 50, 12
    CONTROL          "", IDD_TIME2, "tbtime", WS_BORDER ¦
                     WS_TABSTOP ¦ 0x5000,
                     217, 44, 50, 12
    CONTROL          "", IDD_TIME3, "tbtime", WS_BORDER ¦
                     WS_TABSTOP ¦ 0xA000,
                     217, 64, 50, 12
    CONTROL          "", IDD_TIME4, "tbtime", WS_BORDER ¦
                     WS_TABSTOP ¦ 0x6000,
                     217, 84, 50, 12
    DEFPUSHBUTTON    "OK", IDOK, 121, 122, 44, 14
    CONTROL          "Date", -1, "tbImprint", 0x5201, 9,
                     14, 124, 94
    CONTROL          "Time", -1, "tbImprint", 0x5201,
                     152, 14, 124, 94
END

ID_FLOATINT DIALOG 33, 10, 235, 135
STYLE WS_POPUP ¦ WS_CAPTION
CAPTION "Float and Integer Class Example"
BEGIN
    CONTROL          "Integer", 3011, "tbImprint",
                     0x5240, 9, 8, 72, 96
    CONTROL          "99999999", IDD_INT1, "tbinteger",
                     WS_BORDER ¦
                     WS_TABSTOP, 20, 19, 50, 12
```

```
    CONTROL         "99999999", IDD_INT2, "tbinteger",
                    WS_BORDER ¦
                    WS_TABSTOP ¦ 0x3000, 20, 35, 50, 12
    CONTROL         "999", IDD_INT3, "tbinteger",
                    WS_BORDER ¦ WS_TABSTOP, 20,
                    51, 50, 12
    CONTROL         "99", IDD_INT4, "tbinteger",
                    WS_BORDER ¦ WS_TABSTOP, 20,
                    67, 50, 12
    CONTROL         "Float", 3012, "tbImprint", 0x5240,
                    96, 8, 130, 96
    LTEXT           "FS_MONEY", -1, 104, 21, 53, 8, NOT
                    WS_GROUP
    LTEXT           "FS_SEPARATOR", -1, 104, 37, 56, 8,
                    NOT WS_GROUP
    CONTROL         "99999999.99", IDD_FLOAT1,
                    "tbfloat", WS_BORDER ¦
                    WS_TABSTOP ¦ 0x1000, 167, 19, 50, 12
    CONTROL         "9999999.99", IDD_FLOAT2, "tbfloat",
                    WS_BORDER ¦
                    WS_TABSTOP ¦ 0x3000, 167, 35, 50, 12
    CONTROL         "99999.9999", IDD_FLOAT3, "tbfloat",
                    WS_BORDER ¦
                    WS_TABSTOP, 167, 51, 50, 12
    CONTROL         "999.99", IDD_FLOAT4, "tbfloat",
                    WS_BORDER ¦ WS_TABSTOP,
                    167, 67, 50, 12
    CONTROL         "99.9", IDD_FLOAT5, "tbfloat",
                    WS_BORDER ¦ WS_TABSTOP,
                    167, 83, 50, 12
    DEFPUSHBUTTON   "OK", IDOK, 95, 114, 44, 14
END
```

Listing A.3. Resource definition file (POWER.RC).

```
#include <windows.h>
#include "powerpak.h"
#include "dialog.h"
#include "resource.h"

IDI_POWER ICON     powerpak.ico
FpLogo1  VIEWPICT Fplogo1.pcx
FpLogo2  VIEWPICT Fplogo2.pcx
```

continues

LISTING A.3. CONTINUED

```
FpLogo3  VIEWPICT Fplogo3.pcx
FpLogo4  VIEWPICT Fplogo4.pcx
FpLogo5  VIEWPICT Fplogo5.pcx
FpLogo6  VIEWPICT Fplogo6.pcx
FpLogo7  VIEWPICT Fplogo7.pcx
FpLogo8  VIEWPICT Fplogo8.pcx

IDM_MENU MENU
   BEGIN
   POPUP "&File"
      BEGIN
      MENUITEM  "System &Functions...", IDM_FILE_SYSFUNC
      MENUITEM  "File &Copy...",        IDM_FILE_FILECOPY
      MENUITEM SEPARATOR
      MENUITEM "&About...",             IDM_FILE_ABOUT
      MENUITEM SEPARATOR
      MENUITEM "E&xit",                 IDM_FILE_EXIT
      END

   POPUP "&Examples"
      BEGIN
      MENUITEM "&Travel Example..." ,   IDM_EDIT_TRAVEL
      MENUITEM "&DateTime...",          IDM_EDIT_DATETIME
      MENUITEM "&FloatInt...",          IDM_EDIT_FLOATINT
      MENUITEM "&Imprint...",           IDM_MISC_IMPRINT
      MENUITEM "&Progress Bar...",      IDM_MISC_PROGRESS
      MENUITEM "&View Text...",         IDM_MISC_VIEWTEXT
      END

   POPUP "&Music"
      BEGIN
      MENUITEM "&Start Song",           IDM_PLAY_START
      MENUITEM "Sto&p Song",            IDM_PLAY_STOP
      END

END

STRINGTABLE
   BEGIN
   IDS_CLASSNAME          "PowerDemo"
   IDS_WINDOWTITLE     "Windows Programmer's Power Pack"
   END

rcinclude power.dlg
```

LISTING A.4. MODULE DEFINITION FILE (POWER.DEF).

```
NAME           POWER

DESCRIPTION    'POWER'

STUB           'WINSTUB.EXE'

EXETYPE        WINDOWS

CODE           LOADONCALL MOVEABLE DISCARDABLE
DATA           MOVEABLE MULTIPLE PRELOAD

HEAPSIZE       8096
STACKSIZE      8192

SEGMENTS
    ABOUT_TEXT      MOVEABLE DISCARDABLE LOADONCALL
    DATETIME_TEXT   MOVEABLE DISCARDABLE LOADONCALL
    FILECOPY_TEXT   MOVEABLE DISCARDABLE LOADONCALL
    FLOATINT_TEXT   MOVEABLE DISCARDABLE LOADONCALL
    IMPRINT_TEXT    MOVEABLE DISCARDABLE LOADONCALL
    INIT_TEXT       MOVEABLE DISCARDABLE PRELOAD
    PLAY_TEXT       MOVEABLE DISCARDABLE LOADONCALL
    POWER_TEXT      MOVEABLE             PRELOAD
    PROGRESS_TEXT   MOVEABLE DISCARDABLE LOADONCALL
    SYSFUNC_TEXT    MOVEABLE DISCARDABLE LOADONCALL
    TRAVEL_TEXT     MOVEABLE DISCARDABLE LOADONCALL
    VIEW_TEXT       MOVEABLE DISCARDABLE LOADONCALL
    WINMAIN_TEXT    MOVEABLE             PRELOAD
    _TEXT           MOVEABLE             PRELOAD

EXPORTS
        MainWndProc      @1
        DlgImprintProc   @2
        DlgProgressProc  @3
        ViewDemoProc     @4
        DlgAboutProc     @5
        SysFuncProc      @6
        TravelWndProc    @7
        FileCopyWndProc  @8
        DateTimeWndProc  @9
        FloatIntWndProc  @10
```

Listing A.5. Application header file (POWER.H).

```
#include <windows.h>
#include <powerpak.h>
#include <stdlib.h>
#include <stdio.h>
#include <string.h>
#include <ctype.h>
#include <malloc.h>
#include <math.h>
#include "dialog.h"
#include "resource.h"

#ifndef MAIN
#define EXTERN extern
#else
#define EXTERN
#endif

#define SZCLASSNAME 40
#define SZWINDOWTITLE 80

EXTERN HANDLE   hInst;
EXTERN COLORREF ColorDlgBkgrnd;
EXTERN HBRUSH   hBrushDlgBkgrnd;
EXTERN HWND     hwnd;
EXTERN HWND     hViewDemo;

BOOL InitApplication(HINSTANCE hInstance);
BOOL InitInstance (HINSTANCE hInstance, int nCmdShow);
LRESULT CALLBACK MainWndProc(HWND hWnd, UINT message,
    WPARAM wParam, LPARAM lParam);

LRESULT CALLBACK DlgAboutProc(HWND hWnd, UINT message,
    WPARAM wParam, LPARAM lParam);
LRESULT CALLBACK DlgImprintProc(HWND hWnd, UINT message,
    WPARAM wParam, LPARAM lParam);
LRESULT CALLBACK DlgProgressProc(HWND hWnd,
                                 UINT message,
    WPARAM wParam, LPARAM lParam);
LRESULT CALLBACK ViewDemoProc(HWND hWnd, UINT message,
    WPARAM wParam, LPARAM lParam);
LRESULT CALLBACK TravelWndProc(HWND hWnd, UINT message,
    WPARAM wParam, LPARAM lParam);
LRESULT CALLBACK SysFuncProc(HWND hWnd, UINT message,
    WPARAM wParam, LPARAM lParam);
```

```
LRESULT CALLBACK FileCopyWndProc(HWND hDlg,
                                 UINT message,
    WPARAM wParam, LPARAM lParam);
LRESULT CALLBACK FloatIntWndProc(HWND hDlg,
                                 UINT message,
    WPARAM wParam, LPARAM lParam);
LRESULT CALLBACK DateTimeWndProc(HWND hDlg,
                                 UINT message,
    WPARAM wParam, LPARAM lParam);

VOID DemoSysFunc(HWND hWnd);
VOID DemoFileCopy(HWND hWnd);
VOID Travel(HWND hWnd);
VOID FloatInt(HWND hWnd);
VOID DateTime(HWND hWnd);
BOOL ViewDemo(HWND hWnd);
BOOL RegisterViewDemo(HINSTANCE hInstance);
VOID PlayStartSong(HWND hWnd);
VOID PlayStopSong(VOID);
```

LISTING A.6. DIALOG HEADER FILE (DIALOG.H).

```
#define ID_ABOUTBOX          100
#define IDD_ABOUT_LOGO       101

#define ID_IMPRINT               200
#define IDD_IMPRINT_OUT          201
#define IDD_IMPRINT_IN           202
#define IDD_IMPRINT_GROUPBOX     203
#define IDD_IMPRINT_OUTFRAME     204
#define IDD_IMPRINT_INFRAME      205
#define IDD_IMPRINT_LINESIN      206
#define IDD_IMPRINT_LINESOUT     207
#define IDD_IMPRINT_OK           208

#define ID_PROGRESS                  300
#define IDD_PROGRESS_HPROGRESS       301
#define IDD_PROGRESS_HPROGRESSLEFT   302
#define IDD_PROGRESS_HPROGRESSRIGHT 303
#define IDD_PROGRESS_VPROGRESS       304
#define IDD_PROGRESS_VPROGRESSLEFT   305
#define IDD_PROGRESS_VPROGRESSRIGHT 306
```

continues

Listing A.6. continued

```
#define ID_SYSFUNCS          400
#define IDD_FREEMEM          401
#define IDD_NODRIVES         402
#define IDD_FIXEDDRIVES      403
#define IDD_NETWORKDRIVES    404
#define IDD_CURRENTDRIVE     405
#define IDD_TOTALSPACE       406
#define IDD_FREESPACE        407
#define IDD_PERCENTFULL      408

#define ID_FILECOPY          500
#define IDD_FILECOPYSRC      501
#define IDD_FILECOPYDST      502
#define IDD_FILECOPY         503

#define ID_TRAVEL            600
#define IDD_STARTDATE        601
#define IDD_ENDDATE          602
#define IDD_VAL1             603
#define IDD_VAL2             604
#define IDD_VAL3             605
#define IDD_VAL4             606
#define IDD_VAL5             607

#define ID_DATETIME          700
#define IDD_DATE1            701
#define IDD_DATE2            702
#define IDD_DATE3            703
#define IDD_DATE4            704
#define IDD_DATE5            705
#define IDD_TIME1            706
#define IDD_TIME2            707
#define IDD_TIME3            708
#define IDD_TIME4            709

#define ID_FLOATINT          800
#define IDD_FLOAT1           801
#define IDD_FLOAT2           802
#define IDD_FLOAT3           803
#define IDD_FLOAT4           804
#define IDD_FLOAT5           805
#define IDD_INT1             806
#define IDD_INT2             807
```

```
#define IDD_INT3            808
#define IDD_INT4            809
```

Listing A.7. Resource header file (RESOURCE.H).

```
#define IDM_MENU                1
#define IDI_POWER               1

#define IDM_FILE_SYSFUNC        100
#define IDM_FILE_FILECOPY       101
#define IDM_FILE_SYSTIME        102
#define IDM_FILE_ABOUT          103
#define IDM_FILE_EXIT           104
#define IDM_EDIT_TRAVEL         105
#define IDM_EDIT_DATETIME       106
#define IDM_EDIT_FLOATINT       107
#define IDM_MISC_IMPRINT        108
#define IDM_MISC_PROGRESS       109
#define IDM_MISC_VIEWTEXT       110
#define IDM_PLAY_START          111
#define IDM_PLAY_STOP           112

#define  IDS_CLASSNAME          1
#define  IDS_WINDOWTITLE        2
```

Listing A.8. Source code module (ABOUT.C).

```
#include "power.h"

/*******************************************************/
/* Function: DlgAboutProc
*/
/* Purpose: Callback function for about box.
*/
/* Returns: TRUE/FALSE
/*******************************************************/
LRESULT CALLBACK DlgAboutProc(HWND hWnd, UINT Msg,
    WPARAM wParam, LPARAM lParam)
    {
    VIEWPICT_ANIMATE AnimateLogo;
    HCURSOR          hCursor;
```

continues

LISTING A.8. CONTINUED

```
    static VIEWPICT_ANIMATEPICT AnimatePictLogo[] =
      {
     (LPSTR)"FpLogo1", VPS_RESOURCE ¦
          VPS_PCX, 0, 0, VIEWPICT_DEFDELAY,
     (LPSTR)"FpLogo2", VPS_RESOURCE ¦
          VPS_PCX, 0, 0, VIEWPICT_DEFDELAY,
     (LPSTR)"FpLogo3", VPS_RESOURCE ¦
          VPS_PCX, 0, 0, VIEWPICT_DEFDELAY,
     (LPSTR)"FpLogo4", VPS_RESOURCE ¦
          VPS_PCX, 0, 0, VIEWPICT_DEFDELAY,
     (LPSTR)"FpLogo5", VPS_RESOURCE ¦
          VPS_PCX, 0, 0, VIEWPICT_DEFDELAY,
     (LPSTR)"FpLogo6", VPS_RESOURCE ¦
          VPS_PCX, 0, 0, VIEWPICT_DEFDELAY,
     (LPSTR)"FpLogo7", VPS_RESOURCE ¦
          VPS_PCX, 0, 0, VIEWPICT_DEFDELAY,
     (LPSTR)"FpLogo8", VPS_RESOURCE ¦
          VPS_PCX, 0, 0, VIEWPICT_DEFDELAY,
     };

   switch(Msg)
       {
       case WM_INITDIALOG:
           AnimateLogo.AnimateHdr.PictureCnt =
               sizeof(AnimatePictLogo) /
               sizeof(VIEWPICT_ANIMATEPICT);
           AnimateLogo.AnimateHdr.TimeDelay = 150;
           AnimateLogo.AnimatePict = AnimatePictLogo;

           hCursor = SetCursor(LoadCursor(NULL,
                                IDC_WAIT));
           ShowCursor(TRUE);

           SendDlgItemMessage(hWnd, IDD_ABOUT_LOGO,
            VPM_SETFRAMES,0,(LONG)(LPSTR)&AnimateLogo);

           ShowCursor(FALSE);
           SetCursor(hCursor);
           return (TRUE);

       case WM_CTLCOLOR:
           if (HIWORD(lParam) == CTLCOLOR_DLG)
               return (hBrushDlgBkgrnd);

           else if (HIWORD(lParam) == CTLCOLOR_STATIC
                   ¦¦
```

```
                HIWORD(lParam) == CTLCOLOR_TBVIEWPICT)
                {
                SetBkColor(wParam, ColorDlgBkgrnd);
                return (hBrushDlgBkgrnd);
                }
            return FALSE;

        case WM_COMMAND:
            switch (wParam)
                {
                case IDOK:
                case IDCANCEL:
                    EndDialog(hWnd, 0);
                    break;
                default:
                    return (FALSE);
                }
            break;
        }
    return (FALSE);
  }
```

LISTING A.9. SOURCE CODE MODULE (DATETIME.C).

```
#include "power.h"

static BOOL Command(HWND hWnd, WPARAM wParam, LPARAM
                    lParam);

/*****************************************************/
/* Function: DateTime
*/
/* Purpose: Creates the DateTime Dialog Box
*/
/*****************************************************/
VOID DateTime(HWND hWnd)
    {
    FARPROC lpProc;

    lpProc = MakeProcInstance((FARPROC)DateTimeWndProc,
                              hInst);
```

continues

LISTING A.9. CONTINUED

```
    DialogBox(hInst, MAKEINTRESOURCE(ID_DATETIME), hWnd,
             lpProc);
    FreeProcInstance (lpProc);
    }
/*********************************************************/
/* Function: DateTimeWndProc
*/
/* Purpose: Callback function for DateTime dialog box
*/
/* Returns: TRUE/FALSE
*/
/*********************************************************/
LRESULT CALLBACK DateTimeWndProc(HWND hDlg,
                                  UINT message,
    WPARAM wParam, LPARAM lParam)
    {
    switch(message)
        {
        case WM_INITDIALOG:
            return TRUE;

        case WM_CTLCOLOR:
            if(HIWORD(lParam) == CTLCOLOR_DLG)
                return hBrushDlgBkgrnd;

            else if (HIWORD(lParam) == CTLCOLOR_STATIC
                     ||
                     HIWORD(lParam) == CTLCOLOR_TBEDIT)
                {
                SetBkColor(wParam, ColorDlgBkgrnd);
                return hBrushDlgBkgrnd;
                }
            break;

        case WM_COMMAND:
            if(Command (hDlg, wParam, lParam))
                return TRUE;
            break;
        }
    return FALSE;
    }
```

```
/*****************************************************/
/* Function: Command
*/
/* Purpose: Handles WM_COMMAND messages
*/
/* Returns: TRUE/FALSE
*/
/*****************************************************/
BOOL Command(HWND hWnd, WPARAM wParam, LPARAM lParam)
    {
    switch(wParam)
        {
        case IDOK:
        case IDCANCEL:
            EndDialog(hWnd, FALSE);
            break;

        default:
            return FALSE;
        }
    return TRUE;
    }
```

LISTING A.10. SOURCE CODE MODULE (FILECOPY.C).

```
#include "power.h"

static VOID ExecFileCopy(HWND hDlg);
static VOID PaintItem(LPDRAWITEMSTRUCT lpData);
static VOID FileCopyCommand(HWND hDlg,
    WPARAM wParam, LPARAM lParam);
static VOID FileCopyInit(HWND hDlg);

/*****************************************************/
/* Function: DemoFileCopy
*/
/* Purpose: Creates the copy file dialog box
*/
/*****************************************************/
VOID DemoFileCopy(HWND hWnd)
    {
    FARPROC    lpProc;
```

continues

LISTING A.10. CONTINUED

```
    lpProc = MakeProcInstance((FARPROC)FileCopyWndProc,
                              hInst);
    if(lpProc)
        {
        DialogBox(hInst, MAKEINTRESOURCE(ID_FILECOPY),
                  hWnd, lpProc);
        FreeProcInstance(lpProc);
        }
    }
/*******************************************************/
/* Function: FileCopyCommand
*/
/* Purpose: Handles WM_COMMAND messages for copy file
/* dialog box
/*******************************************************/
static VOID FileCopyCommand(HWND hDlg, WPARAM wParam,
                            LPARAM lParam)
    {
    switch(wParam)
        {
        case IDD_FILECOPY:
            ExecFileCopy(hDlg);
            break;

        case IDOK:
        case IDCANCEL:
            EndDialog(hDlg, FALSE);
            break;
        }
    }

/*******************************************************/
/* Function: ExecFileCopy
*/
/* Purpose: Copies a file
*/
/*******************************************************/
static VOID ExecFileCopy(HWND hDlg)
    {
    char  src[PATHLEN+1];
    char  dst[PATHLEN+1];

    src[0] = '\0';
    dst[0] = '\0';
    GetDlgItemText(hDlg, IDD_FILECOPYSRC, (LPSTR)src,
                   PATHLEN);
```

```
    GetDlgItemText(hDlg, IDD_FILECOPYDST, (LPSTR)dst,
                   PATHLEN);
    if(StrLen(dst) && StrLen(src))
        FileMultipleCopy(src, dst);
    }

/*******************************************************/
/* Function: FileCopyInit
*/
/* Purpose: Initializes copy file dialog box controls
*/
/*******************************************************/
static VOID FileCopyInit(HWND hDlg)
    {
    SendDlgItemMessage(hDlg, IDD_FILECOPYSRC,
        EM_LIMITTEXT, PATHLEN, 0l);
    SendDlgItemMessage(hDlg, IDD_FILECOPYDST,
        EM_LIMITTEXT, PATHLEN, 0l);
    }

/*******************************************************/
/* Function: FileCopyWndProc
*/
/* Purpose: Callback function for filecopy dialog box.
*/
/* Returns: FALSE
*/
/*******************************************************/
LRESULT CALLBACK FileCopyWndProc(HWND hDlg,
                                 UINT message,
    WPARAM wParam, LPARAM lParam)
    {
    switch(message)
        {
        case WM_INITDIALOG:
            FileCopyInit(hDlg);
            return TRUE;
            break;

        case WM_COMMAND:
            FileCopyCommand(hDlg, wParam, lParam);
            break;
        }
    return FALSE;
    }
```

Listing A.11. Source code module (FLOATINT.C).

```
#include "power.h"

static VOID InitDlg(HWND);
static BOOL Command(HWND hWnd, WPARAM wParam, LPARAM
                    lParam);

/*****************************************************/
/* Function: FloatInt
*/
/* Purpose: Creates the FloatInt Dialog Box.
*/
/*****************************************************/
VOID FloatInt(HWND hWnd)
    {
    FARPROC lpProc;

    lpProc = MakeProcInstance((FARPROC)FloatIntWndProc,
                              hInst);
    DialogBox(hInst, MAKEINTRESOURCE(ID_FLOATINT), hWnd,
              lpProc);

    FreeProcInstance(lpProc);
    }

/*****************************************************/
/* Function: FloatIntWndProc
*/
/* Purpose: Callback function for FloatInt Dialog Box
*/
/* Returns: TRUE/FALSE
*/
/*****************************************************/
LRESULT CALLBACK FloatIntWndProc(HWND hDlg,
    UINT message,
    WPARAM wParam, LPARAM lParam)
    {
    switch(message)
        {
        case WM_INITDIALOG:
            InitDlg(hDlg);
            return TRUE;

        case WM_CTLCOLOR:
            if(HIWORD(lParam) == CTLCOLOR_DLG)
                return hBrushDlgBkgrnd;
```

```
            else if(HIWORD(lParam) == CTLCOLOR_STATIC ¦¦
                    HIWORD(lParam) == CTLCOLOR_TBEDIT)
                {
                SetBkColor(wParam, ColorDlgBkgrnd);
                return hBrushDlgBkgrnd;
                }

            break;

        case WM_COMMAND:
            return Command(hDlg, wParam, lParam);
        }
    return FALSE;
    }

/*****************************************************/
/* Function: Command
*/
/* Purpose: Processes the WM_COMMAND message for
/* FloatInt Dlg
/* Returns: TRUE/FALSE
*/
/*****************************************************/
BOOL Command(HWND hWnd, WPARAM wParam, LPARAM lParam)
    {
    switch (wParam)
        {
        case IDOK:
        case IDCANCEL:
            EndDialog (hWnd, FALSE);
            break;

        default:
            return FALSE;
        }
    return TRUE;
    }

/*****************************************************/
/* Function: InitDlg
*/
/* Purpose: Performs initialization of FloatInt Dlg Box
*/
/*****************************************************/
```

continues

Listing A.11. continued

```
VOID InitDlg(HWND hDlg)
    {
    FloatSetRange(GetDlgItem(hDlg,IDD_FLOAT1),
        (double)0.0,(double)10000000.00);
    FloatSetRange(GetDlgItem(hDlg,IDD_FLOAT2),
        (double)0.0,(double)5200000.00);
    FloatSetRange(GetDlgItem(hDlg,IDD_FLOAT3),
        (double)0.0,(double)99999.9911);
    FloatSetRange(GetDlgItem(hDlg,IDD_FLOAT4),
        (double)0.0,(double)999.99);
    FloatSetRange(GetDlgItem(hDlg,IDD_FLOAT5),
        (double)-99.0,(double)99.5);

    IntSetRange(GetDlgItem(hDlg,IDD_INT1),
        (LONG)0,(LONG)52000000);
    IntSetRange(GetDlgItem(hDlg,IDD_INT2),
        (LONG)0,(LONG)10000000);
    IntSetRange(GetDlgItem(hDlg,IDD_INT3),
        (LONG)0,(LONG)9999);
    IntSetRange(GetDlgItem(hDlg,IDD_INT4),
        (LONG)-99,(LONG)99);

    IntSetSpin(GetDlgItem(hDlg, IDD_INT1),
        TRUE, FALSE, 5);
    IntSetSpin(GetDlgItem(hDlg, IDD_INT2),
        FALSE, 0, 0);
    }
```

Listing A.12. Source code module (IMPRINT.C).

```
#include "power.h"

/*********************************************************/
/* Function: DlgImprintProc
*/
/* Purpose: Callback function for Imprint Dialog box.
*/
/* Returns: TRUE/FALSE
*/
/*********************************************************/
LRESULT CALLBACK DlgImprintProc(HWND hWnd, UINT Msg,
    WPARAM wParam, LPARAM lParam)
    {
```

```
static HBRUSH hBrush;

switch(Msg)
    {
    case WM_INITDIALOG:
        hBrush =
            CreateSolidBrush(RGBCOLOR_PALEGRAY);

        SendDlgItemMessage(hWnd,
            IDD_IMPRINT_LINESIN,
            IM_SETLINECNT, 0, MAKELONG(2, 3));

        SendDlgItemMessage(hWnd,
            IDD_IMPRINT_LINESOUT,
            IM_SETLINECNT, 0, MAKELONG(2, 3));

        {
        IMPRINTCOLOR ImprintColor;

        SendDlgItemMessage(hWnd,
            IDD_IMPRINT_OUTFRAME,
            IM_GETCOLOR, 0,
            (LONG)(LPSTR)&ImprintColor);

        ImprintColor.ColorFrame = RGBCOLOR_RED;

        SendDlgItemMessage(hWnd,
            IDD_IMPRINT_OUTFRAME,
            IM_SETCOLOR, 0,
            (LONG)(LPSTR)&ImprintColor);
        }
        return TRUE;

    case WM_CTLCOLOR:
        if(HIWORD(lParam) == CTLCOLOR_DLG)
            return (hBrush);

        else if(HIWORD(lParam) == CTLCOLOR_STATIC)
            {
            SetBkColor(wParam, RGBCOLOR_PALEGRAY);
            return (hBrush);
            }
        break;

    case WM_DESTROY:
        DeleteObject(hBrush);
```

continues

Listing A.12. continued

```
            break;

        case WM_COMMAND:
            switch(wParam)
                {
                case IDD_IMPRINT_OK:
                case IDOK:
                case IDCANCEL:
                    EndDialog(hWnd, FALSE);
                    return FALSE;
                }
           break;
        }
    return (FALSE);
    }
```

Listing A.13. Source code module (INIT.C).

```
#include "power.h"

/*******************************************************/
/* Function: InitApplication
*/
/* Purpose: Performs all intialization for first
*/ instance of app.
/* Returns: TRUE if successful, FALSE if failure.
*/
/*******************************************************/
BOOL InitApplication(HINSTANCE hInstance)
    {
    BOOL bResult;
    char szClassName[SZCLASSNAME];
    WNDCLASS wc;

    /* Load the window class name from resource string
       table */

    if(!LoadString(hInstance, IDS_CLASSNAME,
        szClassName, sizeof szClassName))
        return FALSE;

    /* Class styles */
```

```
    wc.style         = 0;
    /* Name of message loop function for windows of this
       class  */
    wc.lpfnWndProc   = MainWndProc;
    /* Not using Class Extra data */
    wc.cbClsExtra    = 0;
    /* Not using Window Extra data */
    wc.cbWndExtra    = 0;
    /* Instance that owns this class */
    wc.hInstance     = hInstance;
    /* Use default application icon  */
    wc.hIcon         = LoadIcon(hInstance,
         MAKEINTRESOURCE(IDI_POWER));
    /* Use arrow cursor  */
    wc.hCursor       = LoadCursor(NULL, IDC_ARROW);
    /* Use system background color */
    wc.hbrBackground = GetStockObject(WHITE_BRUSH);
    /* Resource name for menu */
    wc.lpszMenuName  = MAKEINTRESOURCE(IDM_MENU);
    /* name given to this class */
    wc.lpszClassName = szClassName;

    /* Register the window class */
    bResult = RegisterClass(&wc);

    /* return result based on registration */
    return bResult;
    }

/*****************************************************/
/* Function: InitInstance
*/
/* Purpose: Performs all initialization for all
*/ instances of app.
/* Returns: TRUE if successful, FALSE if failure.
*/
/*****************************************************/
BOOL InitInstance (HINSTANCE hInstance, int nCmdShow)
    {
    char szClassName[SZCLASSNAME];
    char szWindowTitle[SZWINDOWTITLE];

    hInst = hInstance;

    /* Load the window class name from resource string
       table */
```

continues

LISTING A.13. CONTINUED

```
    if(!LoadString(hInst, IDS_CLASSNAME,
        szClassName, sizeof szClassName))
        return FALSE;
    /* Load the window title from resource string table */
    if(!LoadString(hInst, IDS_WINDOWTITLE,
        szWindowTitle, sizeof szWindowTitle))
        return FALSE;

    hwnd = CreateWindow(szClassName,/* window class */
                        szWindowTitle,/* text for title
                                         bar */
                        WS_OVERLAPPEDWINDOW,/* style(s)  */
                        CW_USEDEFAULT,/* default x  pos  */
                        CW_USEDEFAULT,/* default y  pos  */
                        CW_USEDEFAULT,/* default cx pos  */
                        CW_USEDEFAULT,/* default cy pos  */
                        0,             /* parent window   */
                        0,             /* menu            */
                        hInstance,     /* owning instance */
                        NULL);         /* user defined
                                          params*/

    /* if CreateWindow wasn't successful - return false */
    if(!hwnd)
        return FALSE;

    /* show and paint window */
    ShowWindow(hwnd, nCmdShow);
    UpdateWindow(hwnd);

    return TRUE;

    }
```

LISTING A.14. SOURCE CODE MODULE (PLAY.C).

```
#include "power.h"

char TestSong[] = "LAG1EC2SG1SD2SG1SE- \
2SG1SC2SG1SD2SG1SE-\
2SG1SF2SG1SD2SG1SE-2SG1SF2SG1SG2SG1SE- \
2SG1SF2SG1SG2SG1SA-\
```

```
2SG1SF2SG1SG2SG1SE-2SG1SF2SG1SD2SG1SE- \
2SG1SC2SG1SD2SG1SB1\
SG1SC2SG1SG1EA-1SG1SF1SG1SG1TG+1TG1TG+1TG1TG+1TG1TG+ \
1TG1SR1E<AX";

HANDLE hPlayInst;

VOID PlayStartSong(HWND hWnd)
    {
    ToneInit();
    hPlayInst = Play(hWnd, TestSong, 3);
    }


VOID PlayStopSong()
    {
    PlayStop(hPlayInst);
    }
```

Listing A.15. Source code module (POWER.C).

```
#include "power.h"

/*******************************************************/
/* Function: MainWndProc
*/
/* Purpose: Processes messages for main window
*/
/* Returns: Varies
*/
/*******************************************************/
LRESULT CALLBACK MainWndProc(HWND hWnd, UINT message,
    WPARAM wParam, LPARAM lParam)
    {
    FARPROC             ProcInst;

    switch(message)
        {
        case WM_CREATE:
            return FALSE;

        case WM_COMMAND:
            switch((WORD)wParam)
                {
                case IDM_FILE_SYSFUNC:
```

continues

LISTING A.15. CONTINUED

```
                    DemoSysFunc(hWnd);
                    break;

                case IDM_FILE_FILECOPY:
                    DemoFileCopy(hWnd);
                    break;

                case IDM_FILE_ABOUT:
                    ProcInst = MakeProcInstance
                        ((FARPROC)DlgAboutProc, hInst);
                    DialogBoxParam(hInst,
                        MAKEINTRESOURCE(ID_ABOUTBOX),
                        hWnd,ProcInst, 0L);
                    FreeProcInstance(ProcInst);
                    return FALSE;

                case IDM_FILE_EXIT:
                    SendMessage(hWnd, WM_CLOSE, 0, 0L);
                    return FALSE;

                case IDM_EDIT_TRAVEL:
                    Travel(hWnd);
                    break;

                case IDM_EDIT_DATETIME:
                    DateTime(hWnd);
                    break;

                case IDM_EDIT_FLOATINT:
                    FloatInt(hWnd);
                    break;

                case IDM_MISC_IMPRINT:
                    ProcInst = MakeProcInstance
                        ((FARPROC)DlgImprintProc,
                          hInst);
                    DialogBoxParam(hInst,
                        MAKEINTRESOURCE(ID_IMPRINT),
                        hWnd, ProcInst, 0L);
                    FreeProcInstance(ProcInst);
                    return FALSE;

                case IDM_MISC_PROGRESS:
                    ProcInst = MakeProcInstance
                        ((FARPROC)DlgProgressProc,
                         hInst);
```

```
                    DialogBoxParam(hInst,
                        MAKEINTRESOURCE(ID_PROGRESS),
                        hWnd, ProcInst, 0L);
                    FreeProcInstance(ProcInst);
                    return FALSE;

                case IDM_MISC_VIEWTEXT:
                    ViewDemo(hWnd);
                    return FALSE;

                case IDM_PLAY_START:
                    PlayStartSong(hWnd);
                    return FALSE;

                case IDM_PLAY_STOP:
                    PlayStopSong();
                    return FALSE;
                }
            break;

        case WM_DESTROY:
            PostQuitMessage(0);
            return FALSE;

        default:
            return DefWindowProc(hWnd, message, wParam,
                                 lParam);
        }
    return FALSE;
    }
```

LISTING A.16. SOURCE CODE MODULE (PROGRESS.C).

```
#include "power.h"

/****************************************************/
/* Function: DlgProgressProc
*/
/* Purpose: Callback function for the progress
*/ dialog box
/* Returns: TRUE/FALSE
*/
/****************************************************/
```

continues

Listing A.16. continued

```
LRESULT CALLBACK DlgProgressProc(HWND hWnd,
    UINT message,
    WPARAM wParam, LPARAM lParam)
    {
    short Pos;

    lParam;

    switch (message)
        {
        case WM_INITDIALOG:
        SendDlgItemMessage(hWnd, IDD_PROGRESS_HPROGRESS,
                PM_SETRANGE, 0, MAKELONG(0, 5000));

        return TRUE;

        case WM_COMMAND:
            switch(wParam)
                {
                case IDD_PROGRESS_HPROGRESSLEFT:
                    Pos =
                (short)SendDlgItemMessage(hWnd,
                        IDD_PROGRESS_HPROGRESS,
                        PM_GETPOS, 0, 0L);
                    SendDlgItemMessage(hWnd,
                        IDD_PROGRESS_HPROGRESS,
                        PM_SETPOS, Pos - 100, 0L);
                    return FALSE;

                case IDD_PROGRESS_HPROGRESSRIGHT:
                    Pos =
                (short)SendDlgItemMessage(hWnd,
                        IDD_PROGRESS_HPROGRESS,
                        PM_GETPOS, 0, 0L);
                    SendDlgItemMessage(hWnd,
                        IDD_PROGRESS_HPROGRESS,
                        PM_SETPOS,
                        Pos + 100, 0L);
                    return FALSE;

                case IDD_PROGRESS_VPROGRESSLEFT:
                    Pos =
                (short)SendDlgItemMessage(hWnd,
                        IDD_PROGRESS_VPROGRESS,
                        PM_GETPOS, 0, 0L);
```

```
                    SendDlgItemMessage(hWnd,
                        IDD_PROGRESS_VPROGRESS,
                        PM_SETPOS,
                        Pos - 1, 0L);
                    return FALSE;

                case IDD_PROGRESS_VPROGRESSRIGHT:
                    Pos =
                (short)SendDlgItemMessage(hWnd,
                        IDD_PROGRESS_VPROGRESS,
                        PM_GETPOS, 0, 0L);
                    SendDlgItemMessage(hWnd,
                        IDD_PROGRESS_VPROGRESS,
                        PM_SETPOS,
                        Pos + 1, 0L);
                    return FALSE;

                case IDOK:
                case IDCANCEL:
                    EndDialog(hWnd, FALSE);
                return FALSE;
                }
        break;
        }
    return FALSE;
    }
```

LISTING A.17. SOURCE CODE MODULE (SYSFUNC.C).

```
#include "power.h"

#define LINELEN 129

static BOOL DoslibDemo(HWND hDlg);

/*********************************************************/
/* Function: DemoSysFunc
*/
/* Purpose: Creates the SysFuncs dialog box.
*/
/*********************************************************/
VOID DemoSysFunc(HWND hWnd)
    {
```

continues

LISTING A.17. CONTINUED

```
    FARPROC   lpProc;
    int       iValue;

    lpProc = MakeProcInstance((FARPROC)SysFuncProc,
                              hInst);
    iValue = DialogBox(hInst,
        MAKEINTRESOURCE(ID_SYSFUNCS),
        hWnd, lpProc);
    FreeProcInstance(lpProc);
    }

/*****************************************************/
/* Function: SysFuncProc
*/
/* Purpose:  Callback function for SysFuncs dialog box
*/
/* Returns: TRUE/FALSE
*/
/*****************************************************/
LRESULT CALLBACK SysFuncProc(HWND hDlg, UINT message,
    WPARAM wParam, LPARAM lParam)
    {
    int ID;

    switch(message)
        {
        case WM_INITDIALOG:
            DoslibDemo(hDlg);
            return TRUE;

        case WM_COMMAND:
            switch(wParam)
                {
                case IDOK:
                case IDCANCEL:
                    EndDialog( hDlg, FALSE);
                    return TRUE;
                    break;
                default:
                    return FALSE;
                }
             break;

        case WM_CTLCOLOR:
```

```
            if(HIWORD(lParam) == CTLCOLOR_STATIC)
                {
                ID = GetWindowWord (LOWORD(lParam),
                                    GWW_ID);
                if(ID == IDD_NODRIVES ||
                   ID == IDD_FIXEDDRIVES ||
                   ID == IDD_NETWORKDRIVES ||
                   ID == IDD_CURRENTDRIVE ||
                   ID == IDD_TOTALSPACE ||
                   ID == IDD_FREESPACE ||
                   ID == IDD_PERCENTFULL)
                    SetTextColor (wParam, RGB(0,0,255));
                }
            break;

        default:
            return FALSE;
            break;
        }
    return FALSE;
    }

/*******************************************************/
/* Function: DoslibDemo
*/
/* Purpose: Gets the system statistics for SysFunc
*/ Dlg Box
/* Returns: TRUE
*/
/*******************************************************/
BOOL DoslibDemo(HWND hDlg)
    {
    int iNoDrives, iDrive;
    int iFixedDrives, iNetworkDrives, iOtherDrives;
    int iCurrentDrive;
    int iPercentFull;
    DWORD lTotalSpace, lFreeSpace;
    DISKINFO di;
    int iStatus;
    int iDay, iMonth, iYear;

    char szDriveLetter[LINELEN];
    char szNoDrives[LINELEN];
    char szFixedDrives[LINELEN];
    char szNetworkDrives[LINELEN];
    char szOtherDrives[LINELEN];
```

continues

LISTING A.17. CONTINUED

```
    char szTotalSpace[LINELEN];
    char szFreeSpace[LINELEN];
    char szPercentFull[LINELEN];
    char szTitleAndDate[LINELEN];

    if((iNoDrives = SysGetLogicalDriveCount()) == 0)
        return FALSE;

    iFixedDrives = iNetworkDrives = iOtherDrives = 0;
    for(iDrive = 1; iDrive <= iNoDrives; iDrive++)
        {
        if(SysFixedDrive(iDrive))
            iFixedDrives++;
        else
            if(SysNetworkDrive(iDrive))
                iNetworkDrives++;
            else
                iOtherDrives++;
        }

    iCurrentDrive = SysGetDefDrive();

    SysGetDate( &iDay, &iMonth, &iYear);
    StrPrintf( szTitleAndDate, "System Information");

    iStatus = SysDiskInfo( iCurrentDrive, &di);

    lTotalSpace = (DWORD)di.bytesPerSector *
                  (DWORD)di.sectorsPerCluster *
                  (DWORD)di.clustersPerDrive;

    lFreeSpace = (DWORD)di.bytesPerSector *
                 (DWORD)di.sectorsPerCluster *
                 (DWORD)di.availableClusters;

    iPercentFull = (int)(100.0 - ((float)lFreeSpace /
        lTotalSpace) * 100.0);

    szDriveLetter[0] = (char)(iCurrentDrive + 'A' - 1);
    szDriveLetter[1] = NULL;

    sprintf( szNoDrives, "%d", iNoDrives);
    sprintf( szFixedDrives, "%d", iFixedDrives);
    sprintf( szNetworkDrives, "%d", iNetworkDrives);
    sprintf( szOtherDrives, "%d", iOtherDrives);
```

```
    sprintf( szTotalSpace, "%lu bytes", lTotalSpace);
    sprintf( szFreeSpace, "%lu bytes", lFreeSpace);
    sprintf( szPercentFull, "%d", iPercentFull);

    SetDlgItemText(hDlg, IDD_NODRIVES,
        (LPSTR)szNoDrives);
    SetDlgItemText(hDlg, IDD_FIXEDDRIVES,
        (LPSTR)szFixedDrives);
    SetDlgItemText(hDlg, IDD_NETWORKDRIVES,
        (LPSTR)szNetworkDrives);
    SetDlgItemText(hDlg, IDD_CURRENTDRIVE,
        (LPSTR)szDriveLetter);
    SetDlgItemText(hDlg, IDD_TOTALSPACE,
        (LPSTR)szTotalSpace);
    SetDlgItemText(hDlg, IDD_FREESPACE,
        (LPSTR)szFreeSpace);
    SetDlgItemText(hDlg, IDD_PERCENTFULL,
        (LPSTR)szPercentFull);

    SetWindowText(hDlg, (LPSTR)szTitleAndDate);

    return TRUE;
    }
```

Listing A.18. Source code module (TRAVEL.C).

```
#include "power.h"

static VOID InitDlg(HWND hDlg);
static BOOL Command(HWND hWnd, WPARAM wParam, LPARAM
                    lParam);
static VOID DoTotal(HWND hWnd);

/*****************************************************/
/* Function: Travel
*/
/* Purpose: Creates the Travel Dlg Box
*/
/*****************************************************/
VOID Travel(HWND hWnd)
    {
```

continues

LISTING A.18. CONTINUED

```
    FARPROC lpProc;

    lpProc = MakeProcInstance((FARPROC)TravelWndProc,
                              hInst);
    DialogBox(hInst, MAKEINTRESOURCE(ID_TRAVEL), hWnd,
              lpProc);
    FreeProcInstance(lpProc);
    }

/*******************************************************/
/* Function: TravelWndProc
*/
/* Purpose: Callback function for Travel Dlg Box
*/
/* Returns: TRUE/FALSE
*/
/*******************************************************/
LRESULT CALLBACK TravelWndProc(HWND hDlg, UINT message,
    WPARAM wParam, LPARAM lParam)
    {
    switch(message)
        {
        case WM_INITDIALOG:
            InitDlg(hDlg);
            break;

        case WM_CTLCOLOR:
            if(HIWORD(lParam) == CTLCOLOR_DLG)
                return hBrushDlgBkgrnd;

            else if(HIWORD(lParam) == CTLCOLOR_STATIC ¦¦
                    HIWORD(lParam) == CTLCOLOR_TBEDIT)
                {
                SetBkColor(wParam, ColorDlgBkgrnd);
                return hBrushDlgBkgrnd;
                }
            break;

        case WM_COMMAND:
            if(Command (hDlg, wParam, lParam))
                return TRUE;
            break;
        }
    return FALSE;
```

```
    }

/*******************************************************/
/* Function: InitDlg
*/
/* Purpose: Performs initialization for Travel Dlg box.
*/
/*******************************************************/
VOID InitDlg(HWND hDlg)
    {
    FloatSetRange(GetDlgItem(hDlg,IDD_VAL1),
        (double) 0.0,(double)500.00);
    FloatSetRange(GetDlgItem(hDlg,IDD_VAL2),
        (double) 0.0,(double)500.00);
    FloatSetRange(GetDlgItem(hDlg,IDD_VAL3),
        (double) 0.0,(double)500.00);
    FloatSetRange(GetDlgItem(hDlg,IDD_VAL4),
        (double) 0.0,(double)500.00);
    FloatSetRange(GetDlgItem(hDlg,IDD_VAL5),
        (double) 0.0,(double)99999.99);
    SetDlgItemText(hDlg,IDD_VAL5,(LPSTR)"0.0");

    SetFocus(GetDlgItem(hDlg,IDD_STARTDATE));
    }

/*******************************************************/
/* Function: Command
*/
/* Purpose: Processes WM_COMMAND message for Travel
*/ Dlg Box
/* Returns: TRUE/FALSE
*/
/*******************************************************/
BOOL Command(HWND hWnd, WPARAM wParam, LPARAM lParam)
    {
    switch(wParam)
        {
        case IDD_VAL1:
        case IDD_VAL2:
        case IDD_VAL3:
        case IDD_VAL4:
            DoTotal(hWnd);
            break;

        case IDOK:
```

continues

Listing A.18. continued

```
        case IDCANCEL:
            EndDialog(hWnd, FALSE);
            break;
        default:
            return FALSE;
        }
    return TRUE;
    }

/*****************************************************/
/* Function: DoTotal
*/
/* Purpose: Calculates and displays travel expense
*/ totals
/*****************************************************/
VOID DoTotal(HWND hWnd)
    {
    char   szFloatValue[128];
    double dTemp;
    double dTotal = 0.0;

    FloatGetValue(GetDlgItem(hWnd, IDD_VAL1),
                  (LPDOUBLE)&dTemp);
    dTotal += dTemp;

    FloatGetValue(GetDlgItem(hWnd, IDD_VAL2),
                  (LPDOUBLE)&dTemp);
    dTotal += dTemp;

    FloatGetValue(GetDlgItem(hWnd, IDD_VAL3),
                  (LPDOUBLE)&dTemp);
    dTotal += dTemp;

    FloatGetValue(GetDlgItem(hWnd, IDD_VAL4),
                  (LPDOUBLE)&dTemp);
    dTotal += dTemp;

    StrPrintf(szFloatValue, "%f", dTotal);
    SetDlgItemText(hWnd, IDD_VAL5, (LPSTR)szFloatValue);
    }
```

LISTING A.19. SOURCE CODE MODULE (VIEW.C).

```
#include "power.h"

#define IDD_VIEWDEMO 1

LPSTR ViewText[] =
   {
   "Pmt# Date         Rate    Payment   Principal
Interest    Balance Due",
   "-----------------------------------------------------
----------------",
   "1    Jan 01 1991  10.000  $253.63   $170.30   $83.33
$9,829.70",
   "2    Feb 01 1991  10.000  $253.63   $171.72   $81.91
$9,657.98",
   "3    Mar 01 1991  10.000  $253.63   $173.15   $80.48
$9,484.83",
   "4    Apr 01 1991  10.000  $253.63   $174.59   $79.04
$9,310.24",
   "5    May 01 1991  10.000  $253.63   $176.04   $77.59
$9,134.20",
   "6    Jun 01 1991  10.000  $253.63   $177.51   $76.12
$8,956.69",
   "7    Jul 01 1991  10.000  $253.63   $178.99   $74.64
$8,777.70",
   "8    Aug 01 1991  10.000  $253.63   $180.48   $73.15
$8,597.22",
   "9    Sep 01 1991  10.000  $253.63   $181.99   $71.64
$8,415.23",
   "10   Oct 01 1991  10.000  $253.63   $183.50   $70.13
$8,231.73",
   "11   Nov 01 1991  10.000  $253.63   $185.03   $68.60
$8,046.70",
   "12   Dec 01 1991  10.000  $253.63   $186.57   $67.06
$7,860.13",
   "13   Jan 01 1992  10.000  $253.63   $188.13   $65.50
$7,672.00",
   "14   Feb 01 1992  10.000  $253.63   $189.70   $63.93
$7,482.30",
   "15   Mar 01 1992  10.000  $253.63   $191.28   $62.35
$7,291.02",
   "16   Apr 01 1992  10.000  $253.63   $192.87   $60.76
```

continues

LISTING A.19. CONTINUED

```
$7,098.15",
    "17   May 01 1992  10.000  $253.63   $194.48   $59.15
$6,903.67",
    "18   Jun 01 1992  10.000  $253.63   $196.10   $57.53
$6,707.57",
    "19   Jul 01 1992  10.000  $253.63   $197.73   $55.90
$6,509.84",
    "20   Aug 01 1992  10.000  $253.63   $199.38   $54.25
$6,310.46",
    "21   Sep 01 1992  10.000  $253.63   $201.04   $52.59
$6,109.42",
    "22   Oct 01 1992  10.000  $253.63   $202.72   $50.91
$5,906.70",
    "23   Nov 01 1992  10.000  $253.63   $204.41   $49.22
$5,702.29",
    "24   Dec 01 1992  10.000  $253.63   $206.11   $47.52
$5,496.18",
    "25   Jan 01 1993  10.000  $253.63   $207.83   $45.80
$5,288.35",
    "26   Feb 01 1993  10.000  $253.63   $209.56   $44.07
$5,078.79",
    "27   Mar 01 1993  10.000  $253.63   $211.31   $42.32
$4,867.48",
    "28   Apr 01 1993  10.000  $253.63   $213.07   $40.56
$4,654.41",
    "29   May 01 1993  10.000  $253.63   $214.84   $38.79
$4,439.57",
    "30   Jun 01 1993  10.000  $253.63   $216.63   $37.00
$4,222.94",
    "31   Jul 01 1993  10.000  $253.63   $218.44   $35.19
$4,004.50",
    "32   Aug 01 1993  10.000  $253.63   $220.26   $33.37
$3,784.24",
    "33   Sep 01 1993  10.000  $253.63   $222.09   $31.54
$3,562.15",
    "34   Oct 01 1993  10.000  $253.63   $223.95   $29.68
$3,338.20",
    "35   Nov 01 1993  10.000  $253.63   $225.81   $27.82
$3,112.39",
    "36   Dec 01 1993  10.000  $253.63   $227.69   $25.94
$2,884.70",
    "37   Jan 01 1994  10.000  $253.63   $229.59   $24.04
$2,655.11",
    "38   Feb 01 1994  10.000  $253.63   $231.50   $22.13
```

```
$2,423.61",
   "39   Mar 01 1994  10.000  $253.63   $233.43   $20.20
$2,190.18",
   "40   Apr 01 1994  10.000  $253.63   $235.38   $18.25
$1,954.80",
   "41   May 01 1994  10.000  $253.63   $237.34   $16.29
$1,717.46",
   "42   Jun 01 1994  10.000  $253.63   $239.32   $14.31
$1,478.14",
   "43   Jul 01 1994  10.000  $253.63   $241.31   $12.32
$1,236.83",
   "44   Aug 01 1994  10.000  $253.63   $243.32   $10.31
$993.51",
   "45   Sep 01 1994  10.000  $253.63   $245.35    $8.28
$748.16",
   "46   Oct 01 1994  10.000  $253.63   $247.40    $6.23
$500.76",
   "47   Nov 01 1994  10.000  $253.63   $249.46    $4.17
$251.30",
   "48   Dec 01 1994  10.000  $253.39   $251.30    $2.09
$0.00",
   };

BOOL InitViewDemo(HWND hWnd);

/*******************************************************/
/* Function: RegisterViewDemo
*/
/* Purpose: Creates the ViewDemo class
*/
/* Returns: TRUE/FALSE
*/
/*******************************************************/
BOOL RegisterViewDemo(HINSTANCE hInstance)
    {
    WNDCLASS wc;

    wc.style = CS_VREDRAW | CS_HREDRAW;
    wc.lpfnWndProc = ViewDemoProc;
    wc.cbClsExtra = 0;
    wc.cbWndExtra = 0;
    wc.hInstance = hInstance;
    wc.hIcon = LoadIcon(hInstance, "ViewDemo");
    wc.hCursor = LoadCursor(NULL, IDC_ARROW);
```

continues

Listing A.19. continued

```
    wc.hbrBackground = GetStockObject(WHITE_BRUSH);
    wc.lpszMenuName = NULL;
    wc.lpszClassName = "ViewDemo";

    return (RegisterClass(&wc));
    }

/*******************************************************/
/* Function: ViewDemo
*/
/* Purpose: Creates the ViewDemo Window
*/
/* Returns: TRUE/FALSE
*/
/*******************************************************/
BOOL ViewDemo(HWND hWnd)
    {
    hViewDemo = CreateWindow("ViewDemo",
                        "View Demo",
                        WS_OVERLAPPED | WS_SYSMENU |
                        WS_THICKFRAME,
                        CW_USEDEFAULT,
                        CW_USEDEFAULT,
                        CW_USEDEFAULT,
                        CW_USEDEFAULT,
                        hwnd,
                        0,
                        hInst,
                        NULL);
    if(!hViewDemo)
        return FALSE;
    ShowWindow(hViewDemo, SW_SHOWNORMAL);
    UpdateWindow(hViewDemo);

    return TRUE;
    }

/*******************************************************/
/* Function: ViewDemoProc
*/
/* Purpose: Callback function for ViewDemo Window
*/
/* Returns: TRUE/FALSE
*/
/*******************************************************/
```

```
LRESULT CALLBACK ViewDemoProc(HWND hWnd, UINT message,
    WPARAM wParam, LPARAM lParam)
    {
    RECT Rect;
    HWND hWndView;

    switch(message)
        {
        case WM_CREATE:
            GetClientRect(hWnd, &Rect);

            hWndView = CreateWindow("tbViewText",
                                    NULL,
                                    WS_CHILD ¦
                                    WS_VISIBLE,
                                    Rect.left,
                                    Rect.top,
                                    Rect.right,
                                    Rect.bottom,
                                    hWnd,
                                    IDD_VIEWDEMO,
                                    hInst,
                                    NULL);

            if(!hWndView)
                {
                SendMessage(hWnd, WM_CLOSE, 0, 0L);
                return FALSE;
                }

            if(InitViewDemo(hWnd))
                return TRUE;
            return FALSE;

        case WM_SETFOCUS:
            SetFocus(GetDlgItem(hWnd, IDD_VIEWDEMO));
            break;

        case WM_SIZE:
            GetClientRect(hWnd, &Rect);
            MoveWindow(GetDlgItem(hWnd, IDD_VIEWDEMO),
                 Rect.left, Rect.top,
                 Rect.right - Rect.left, Rect.bottom -
                 Rect.top, TRUE);
```

continues

LISTING A.19. CONTINUED

```
            break;

        case WM_COMMAND:
            break;
        }

    return DefWindowProc(hWnd, message, wParam, lParam);
    }

/*****************************************************/
/* Function: InitViewDemo
*/
/* Purpose: Initializes the ViewDemo Window
*/
/* Returns: TRUE/FALSE
*/
/*****************************************************/
BOOL InitViewDemo(HWND hWnd)
    {
    VIEWTEXTCOLOR ViewTextColor;
    short         i;

    ViewTextColor.BackGround    =
        (COLORREF)RGBCOLOR_WHITE;
    ViewTextColor.MainText      =
        (COLORREF)RGBCOLOR_BLUE;
    ViewTextColor.Header        =
        (COLORREF)RGBCOLOR_DEFAULT;
    ViewTextColor.ColTitles     =
        (COLORREF)RGBCOLOR_RED;
    ViewTextColor.RowTitles     =
        (COLORREF)RGBCOLOR_RED;
    ViewTextColor.HighLightText =
        (COLORREF)RGBCOLOR_DEFAULT;
    ViewTextColor.HighLightBk   =
        (COLORREF)RGBCOLOR_DEFAULT;

    SendDlgItemMessage(hWnd, IDD_VIEWDEMO,
                VTM_SETCOLOR,0,
                (LONG)(LPSTR)&ViewTextColor);

    SendDlgItemMessage(hWnd, IDD_VIEWDEMO,
                    VTM_SETCOLHEADERS, 2, 0L);
    SendDlgItemMessage(hWnd, IDD_VIEWDEMO,
                    VTM_SETROWHEADERS, 5, 0L);
```

```
    for(i = 0; i < sizeof(ViewText) / sizeof(LPSTR);
        i++)
        SendDlgItemMessage(hWnd, IDD_VIEWDEMO,
            VTM_ADDSTRING, 0, (LONG)ViewText[i]);

    return TRUE;
    }
```

Listing A.20. Source code module (WINMAIN.C).

```
#define MAIN
#include "power.h"

/*****************************************************/
/* Function: WinMain
*/
/* Purpose: main function for windows app. Initializes
/* all instances of app, translates and
*/ dispatches messages
/* Returns: Value of PostQuitMessage
*/
/*****************************************************/
int PASCAL WinMain(HINSTANCE hInstance, HINSTANCE
                   hPrevInstance,
                   LPSTR lpszCmdLine, int nCmdShow)
    {
    MSG msg;

    RegisterViewDemo(hInstance);

    /* Create Global colors */
    ColorDlgBkgrnd = GetSysColor(COLOR_BTNFACE);
    hBrushDlgBkgrnd = CreateSolidBrush(ColorDlgBkgrnd);

    /* if there isn't a previous instance of app, then*/
    /* initialize the first instance of app.         */
    if(!hPrevInstance)
        if(!InitApplication(hInstance))
            return FALSE;
```

continues

LISTING A.20. CONTINUED

```
    /* perform initialization for all instances of
       application */
    if(!InitInstance(hInstance, nCmdShow))
        return FALSE;

    InitToolBox(hInstance);

    /* Get messages for this application until WM_QUIT
       is received */
    while(GetMessage(&msg, 0, 0, 0))
        {
        TranslateMessage(&msg);
        DispatchMessage(&msg);
        }

    return (int)msg.wParam;
    }
```

Index

E

F

L

M

N-P

Q-R

S

T

U-V

W

Installing the Disk

Windows Programming PowerPack comes with a disk that includes all the source code and files needed to run the programs in this book. To install the disk, follow these steps:

1. Start Microsoft Windows
2. Create a separate directory for the PowerPack.
3. Copy the subdirectories from the disk into that directory.

The four subdirectories are as follows:

DLL
EXAMPLE
INCLUDE
LIB

License Agreement

By opening this package, you are agreeing to be bound by the following agreement.

This software product is copyrighted, and all rights are reserved by the publisher and author. You are licensed to use this software on a single computer. You may copy and/or modify the software as needed to facilitate your use of it on a single computer. Making copies of the software for any other purpose is a violaton of the United States copyright laws.

This software is sold as is without warranty of any kind, either expressed or implied, including but not limited to the implied warranties of merchantability and fitness for a particular purpose. Neither the publisher nor its dealers or distributors assume any liability for any alleged or actual damages arising from the use of this program. (Some states do not allow for the exclusion of implied warranties, so the exclusion may not apply to you.)

What's on the PowerPack Disk?

The PowerPack disk is a subset of Drover's Professional ToolBox for Windows, contained in a single Dynamic Link Library. The aim of this library is to enhance the functionality of the Microsoft Windows Software Development Kit (SDK) and to simplify the task of creating professional, high-quality Windows applications. The PowerPack also interfaces with other development environments, including Actor, WindowsMaker, Borland C++, ToolBook, and SQLWindows.

String Functions

Most of the string functions are C runtime functions that have been rewritten to accept FAR data pointers, allowing them to be easily accessed by small and medium memory model programs.

System Functions

The system functions provide access to system and file-related functions that are not supported by SDK functions. Most of the system functions provide the functionality of MS-DOS Int 21 calls without having to resort to assembly language.

File I/O Functions

As a general rule, buffered file I/O should not be used in Windows programs. Instead, the SDK function *_lopen*, which returns an MS-DOS file handle, should be used to open a file. The ToolBox functions provide enhanced file support using the file handle returned by the *_lopen* call.

Memory Manipulation Functions

Memory manipulation functions are versions of the C runtime memory manipulation calls written to accept FAR and, in some cases, HUGE pointers.

ListBox Functions

List box handling under Windows is completely message-based; that is, adding or locating a string in the list box requires sending one or more messages. These functions perform the same tasks but eliminate the need to explicitly send the messages to the control.

ToolBox Utility and Miscellaneous Functions

The ToolBox utility functions control the behavior of ToolBox itself. Miscellaneous functions are also included in ToolBox.